CHILDREN IN SUDAN

Slaves, Street Children and Child Soldiers

Human Rights Watch/Africa

Human Rights Watch Children's Rights Project

Human Rights Watch
New York • Washington • Los Angeles • London • Brussels

Copyright © September 1995 by Human Rights Watch
All rights reserved.
Printed in the United States of America.

Library of Congress Catalog Card Number: 95-79993
ISBN 1-56432-157-6

Cover photo: Former child soldiers and unaccompanied boys waiting in Lafon for a flight to reunite them with their families, March 1995. Photo by Jemera Rone.

Human Rights Watch/Africa
Human Rights Watch/Africa was established in 1988 to monitor and promote the observance of internationally recognized human rights in sub-Saharan Africa. Janet Fleischman is the Washington director; Alex Vines is the research associate; Kimberly Mazyck is the associate; Alison DesForges, Bronwen Manby, Binaifer Nowrojee and Michele Wagner are consultants. William Carmichael is the chair of the advisory committee and Alice Brown is the vice chair.

Human Rights Watch Children's Rights Project
Human Rights Watch Children's Rights Project was established in 1994 to monitor and promote the human rights of children around the world. Lois Whitman is the director and Mina Samuels is a consultant.

HUMAN RIGHTS WATCH

Human Rights Watch conducts regular, systematic investigations of human rights abuses in some seventy countries around the world. It addresses the human rights practices of governments of all political stripes, of all geopolitical alignments, and of all ethnic and religious persuasions. In internal wars it documents violations by both governments and rebel groups. Human Rights Watch defends freedom of thought and expression, due process and equal protection of the law; it documents and denounces murders, disappearances, torture, arbitrary imprisonment, exile, censorship and other abuses of internationally recognized human rights.

Human Rights Watch began in 1978 with the founding of its Helsinki division. Today, it includes five divisions covering Africa, the Americas, Asia, the Middle East, as well as the signatories of the Helsinki accords. It also includes five collaborative projects on arms transfers, children's rights, free expression, prison conditions, and women's rights. It maintains offices in New York, Washington, Los Angeles, London, Brussels, Moscow, Dushanbe, Rio de Janeiro, and Hong Kong. Human Rights Watch is an independent, nongovernmental organization, supported by contributions from private individuals and foundations worldwide. It accepts no government funds, directly or indirectly.

The staff includes Kenneth Roth, executive director; Cynthia Brown, program director; Holly J. Burkhalter, advocacy director; Robert Kimzey, publications director; Jeri Laber, special advisor; Gara LaMarche, associate director; Lotte Leicht, Brussels Office Director; Juan Méndez, general counsel; Susan Osnos, communications director; Jemera Rone, counsel; Joanna Weschler, United Nations representative; and Derrick Wong, finance and administration director.

The regional directors of Human Rights Watch are José Miguel Vivanco, Americas; Sidney Jones, Asia; Holly Cartner, Helsinki; and Christopher E. George, Middle East. The project directors are Joost R. Hiltermann, Arms Project; Lois Whitman, Children's Rights Project; Gara LaMarche, Free Expression Project; and Dorothy Q. Thomas, Women's Rights Project.

The members of the board of directors are Robert L. Bernstein, chair; Adrian W. DeWind, vice chair; Roland Algrant, Lisa Anderson, Peter D. Bell, Alice L. Brown, William Carmichael, Dorothy Cullman, Irene Diamond, Edith Everett, Jonathan Fanton, Jack Greenberg, Alice H. Henkin, Harold Hongju Koh, Jeh Johnson, Stephen L. Kass, Marina Pinto Kaufman, Alexander MacGregor, Josh Mailman, Andrew Nathan, Jane Olson, Peter Osnos, Kathleen Peratis, Bruce Rabb, Orville Schell, Sid Sheinberg, Gary G. Sick, Malcolm Smith, Nahid Toubia, Maureen White, and Rosalind C. Whitehead.

Addresses for Human Rights Watch
485 Fifth Avenue, New York, NY 10017-6104
Tel: (212) 972-8400, Fax: (212) 972-0905, E-mail: hrwnyc@hrw.org

1522 K Street, N.W., #910, Washington, DC 20005-1202
Tel: (202) 371-6592, Fax: (202) 371-0124, E-mail: hrwdc@hrw.org

10951 West Pico Blvd., #203, Los Angeles, CA 90064-2126
Tel: (310) 475-3070, Fax: (310) 475-5613, E-mail: hrwatchla@igc.apc.org

33 Islington High Street, N1 9LH London, UK
Tel: (171) 713-1995, Fax: (171) 713-1800, E-mail: hrwatchuk@gn.apc.org

15 Rue Van Campenhout, 1040 Brussels, Belgium
Tel: (2) 732-2009, Fax: (2) 732-0471, E-mail: hrwatcheu@gn.apc.org

Gopher Address: gopher.humanrights.org port 5000

CONTENTS

ACKNOWLEDGMENTS vii

GLOSSARY ix

1 SUMMARY AND RECOMMENDATIONS 1
    Arbitrary Arrest and Detention of Street Children 2
    Children Kidnaped From Their Parents and Subjected to Slavery or Forced
        Labor 3
    Military Recruitment for the National Service of Underage Boys and
        Violation of their Freedom of Religion and that of Captured Young
        SPLA Soldiers 4
    Southern Sudan 5
    Recommendations to the Government of Sudan 5
    Recommendations to the SPLM/A and SSIM/A 7
    Recommendations to UNICEF, the ILO, the UNHCR, and others 8
    Recommendation to the U.S., members of the European Union, and other
        concerned countries 8

2 STREET CHILDREN 11
    The Applicable Law 11
        Due Process 11
        Religious Freedom 14
        Right to Preserve Identity 16
    Background 17
    Facilities 21
        Abu Doum Camp for Boys 21
        Soba Camp for Boys 23
        Testimonies from Soba 25
        Dar Bacha'er Home for Girls 27
        Other camps 28
    Recent Improvements 30

3 SLAVERY OR FORCED LABOR OF MINORS KIDNAPED FROM THEIR
    FAMILIES DURING MILITIA RAIDS 31
    The Applicable Law 32
        Slavery 32
        Forced Labor and Child Labor 35

  U.N. Proceedings Against Sudan on Slavery and Forced Labor, and the Government's Response 36
  Group and Individual Cases 40
    Children And Women Captured by Soldiers and PDF Then Freed by Southern Police in Bahr El Ghazal 41
    Alang's Story 43
    "Mabior's" Story 47
    "Akom's" Story 50

4 RECRUITMENT FOR THE NATIONAL MILITARY SERVICE OF UNDERAGE BOYS AND VIOLATION OF THEIR FREEDOM OF RELIGION 54
    "James'" Story 57
    Underage Recruitment from the Soba Street Boys' Camp ... 60
    "Ezekiel's" Story 61

5 TREATMENT OF SPLA CHILD SOLDIERS BY THE GOVERNMENT OF SUDAN 66
    Pochalla Boy Soldiers 66
    Unaccompanied SPLA Boy Soldiers from Cuba Disillusioned in Khartoum 69

6 SOUTHERN SUDAN INDEPENDENCE MOVEMENT/ARMY 77
    "Kuech's" Story 78
    "William's" Story 79
    "Peter's" Story 79

7 SUDAN PEOPLE'S LIBERATION MOVEMENT/ARMY 84

8 CONCLUSION 88

APPENDIX: THE CONVENTION ON THE RIGHTS OF THE CHILD 89

ACKNOWLEDGMENTS

This report was written by Jemera Rone, Counsel to Human Rights Watch. Lois Whitman, Director of the Human Rights Watch Children's Rights Project, edited the report.

Ms. Rone conducted the research for the report with Human Rights Watch Leonard H. Sandler Fellow Brian Owsley during a mission to Khartoum, Sudan, from May 1-June 13, 1995, at the invitation of the Sudanese government. Interviews in Khartoum with nongovernment people and agencies were conducted in private, as agreed with the government before the mission began. The private individuals and groups, however, requested anonymity because of fear of government reprisals, and took great precautions in meeting with us. Interviews in Juba, the largest town in the south, were not private and were controlled by Sudan Security, which terminated the visit before testimony regarding most abuses, including rebel abuses, could be gathered in that town.

Ms. Rone conducted further research in Kenya and southern Sudan from March 5-20, 1995.

GLOSSARY

Dawa Islamiya	Islamic Call, a large Islamic nongovernmental organization that engages in relief work in over fifteen African countries
ICRC	International Committee of the Red Cross
ILO	International Labor Organization
JCC	Juvenile Care Council, a Sudanese organization with government and nongovernment members which operates state facilities for street children
jihad	Holy war (or great struggle or effort, in Islam)
mujahedeen	Holy warriors or participants in *jihad*
murahiliin	Arab tribal militias
National Service	The agency within the Ministry of Defense responsible for conscripting men who under law are obliged to serve one or two years in the armed forces.
NGO	Nongovernmental organization
NIF	National Islamic Front, the militant Islamic political party that came to power in 1989 after a military coup overthrew the elected government
Nuba	The African people living in south Kordofan's Nuba Mountains in Central Sudan; some are Muslims, some Christians, and some practice traditional African religions
OLS	Operation Lifeline Sudan, a joint United Nations/NGO relief operation for internally displaced and famine and war victims in Sudan that began operations in 1989. It serves territory controlled by the government and by the SPLA. Much of its work in southern Sudan is through

	cross-border operations conducted by OLS Southern Sector based in Nairobi.
PDF	Popular Defense Force, a government-sponsored militia. Its training program is designed to produce *mujahedeen* to participate in *jihad*.
SPLM/A	Sudan People's Liberation Movement/Army. The Sudanese rebel movement and army formed in 1983 headed by Commander-in-Chief Dr. John Garang de Mabior. In 1991 a faction split off from the SPLA in protest of Garang's leadership. The Garang or the mainstream group was known thereafter as SPLA-Torit, after its headquarters in Eastern Equatoria, until that town fell to the government in July 1992. It was also known as SPLA-Mainstream, and now as SPLA.
SSIM/A	Southern Sudan Independence Movement/Army. This is the faction of the SPLA, led by Cmdr. Riek Machar Terry Dhurgon, that broke away from the SPLM/A and Dr. John Garang's leadership in August 1991. It was based in Nasir, Upper Nile and for a time was known as "SPLA-Nasir." On March 27, 1993, others joined it and it was renamed "SPLA-United." In November 1994 it was renamed Southern Sudan Independence Movement/Army.
Triple A camps	Displaced persons camps in Ame, Aswa and Atepi, on the East Bank of the Nile in Eastern Equatoria south of Juba, created in 1992 and evacuated in 1994 due to government military advances. These three camps housed up to 100,000 displaced southerners.
TNA	Transitional National Assembly, Sudan's legislative branch, whose members are appointed by the president
UNHCR	United Nations High Commissioner for Refugees
UNICEF	United Nations Children's Fund

1
SUMMARY AND RECOMMENDATIONS

Serious abuses of children's rights continue in Sudan, Africa's largest country, six years after a military coup overthrew the elected civilian government on June 30, 1989, and brought to power a military regime dominated by the National Islamic Front (NIF), a militant Islamist party. The civil war that commenced in 1983 has continued. The rebel Sudan People's Liberation Army (SPLA) seeks a united secular Sudan and autonomy, if not separation, for the African peoples living in the southern third of the country and the Nuba Mountains. The NIF government regards the war as a "holy war" for Islam and its soldiers as "holy warriors," even where the conscripts asked to wage such a war are non-Muslims.

The war has produced an enormous displacement of peoples living in the south and in the Nuba Mountains in central Sudan. More than two million have been displaced to areas of the north, far from the conflict zones, where their African traditions clash with the strict application of Islamic law by the NIF and their religious beliefs are not respected by the Islamic state. Khartoum, the capital city of this country of about 25 million people, now has a population of over four million, and almost half are people displaced by the war.

The children of Sudan, north and south, have been denied their basic rights by all parties to the conflict, and by the government of Sudan even in areas such as Khartoum where there is no war. Many who are considered street children, mostly southerners and Nuba, are removed from their families without notice. They are denied their right to identity when they are given new Arab names and denied their right to freedom of religion when they are subjected to forcible conversion; the government's recent family reunification project may mitigate some damage done to these children.

Some children have been captured in military raids on their villages and taken into household slavery by their captors. Dinka and Nuba children have predominated among those seized and exploited in this way. The government denies the existence of the problem and has made no effort to stop the practice or to punish those who treat Sudanese children as slaves. In addition, underage boys are forcibly recruited into the army or government-sponsored militias, while at the same time the government attempts to focus world attention on the SPLA's use of child soldiers.

The SPLA and SSIA continue to recruit underage soldiers while at the same time the SSIA cooperates with the United Nations Children's Fund (UNICEF) family reunification program.

Arbitrary Arrest and Detention of Street Children

Since 1992 the government has engaged in a campaign of "cleaning up" city streets by rounding up alleged street children and sending them to special, closed camps. Many alleged street children were not street children at all, but were actually living with their families, and were captured while they were running errands such as going to market. These children were, nevertheless, packed off to the closed camps, without any government effort to find out if the child had a family, where it was, and what if any problem caused the child to be out on the street. Thus children have been separated for years and many remain separated from their families.

There are at least three basic human rights problems with the Sudan government's program for street children: 1) the government arbitrarily removes the children from their families without any legal process and holds them in camps for years, usually without notifying their families. Families search for their missing children without any help from authorities; 2) the government does not respect the religious freedom of the children in that it gives them an Islamic religious education whether or not they or their families are Muslims; and 3) the government violates the children's right to their own identity, including their name, when it gives some children new names in Arabic and denies their heritage. These practices, which have been going on for years, violate the United Nations (U.N.) Convention on the Rights of the Child, the African Charter, and the International Covenant on Civil and Political Rights.

Human Rights Watch does not object to social programs to help street children, or to control petty crime. The existence of street children and the problems they face (and that some may cause), however, are not excuses for arbitrary detention and denial of due process, the breakup of families, and the confinement of children in closed camps. These abuses reflect a lack of concern for the individual child that is inconsistent with effective social work, and they violate international law. Moreover, some camps may have been used to warehouse underage boys for military service: one fifteen-year-old boy told Human Rights Watch that he and others were given an option of joining the army or remaining in a camp indefinitely. This warehousing practice is strikingly similar to the practice of the rebel SPLA that the government has long denounced.

While continuing to seize children off the streets of Khartoum, the government has recently undertaken an internationally-funded pilot project designed to reunite children in the camps with their families. This family reunification pilot project took place in Dar Bacha'er (Home of the Future) Home for Girls in Omdurman in 1994, in cooperation with UNICEF, Oxfam/UK and Radda Barnen (Swedish Save the Children). The program involved social work to locate the child's family, investigate its circumstances and the causes of vagrancy, often poverty, and included a project to help the families generate an income. All involved regarded the pilot project as a success.

The government says it intends to expand the program to include the main boys' camp at Abu Doum, the largest of its closed camps, with about 650 boys. While the program could help set right the abuse of unjustly separating these children from their families, it will not make up for the years they spent apart from their families, in substandard facilities, denied the nurture of their kin and the recognition of their own identity, religion, and culture. Nor will it make up for the substantial amount of time and money that families have invested in searching for, and only sometimes finding, their lost children. The first concerns, however, are to institute the return of the children to their families, following upon the project already begun in the girls' camp, and to halt further arbitrary detentions on the past pattern.

Children Kidnaped From Their Parents and Subjected to Slavery or Forced Labor

Many southern and Nuba children have been captured and taken from their families during military raids on their villages by Arab militias and soldiers in the war zones. They are kept for use as unpaid household servants. The soldiers and militia members sometimes take these children with them when they return to their homes in western and northern Sudan, where the children continue to do unpaid labor inside the house or herding animals, on threat of beatings. There have been cases of sexual abuse of these children. There are reports that some are sold.

Army officers, soldiers, militia members, and others operate with total impunity from government prosecution, although their conduct violates laws against kidnaping and forced labor. The Sudan government has failed to live up to its obligations to prevent and punish such abuses under the Convention on the Rights of the Child, the 1926 Slavery Convention as amended, the 1956 Supplementary Convention on the Abolition of Slavery, the 1930 International Labor Organization (ILO) Forced Labor Convention (No. 29) concerning Forced or Compulsory Labor, the 1957 ILO Convention (No. 105) concerning the Abolition of Forced Labor, the African Charter, and the International Covenant on Civil and Political Rights.

The cases we found were of children who were located by their families, or who succeeded in escaping. The families had to undertake the search themselves, with governmental assistance only where they chanced upon southerners among the police officers they met in their search.

It is clear that existing legal remedies are not adequate to promptly free all of the stolen children. While in some cases described below legal procedures (administrative or judicial) eventually led to reunification of the child with his or her family, the legal route is costly and often fruitless.

The government of Sudan flatly denies all allegations of slavery and forced labor. These topics have been under consideration by the ILO, the U.N. Committee on the Rights of Children, the U.N. Commission on Human Rights, and the U.N. Working Group on Contemporary Forms of Slavery for years. The government, however, has never requested the technical assistance and advice that these agencies have suggested could be used to pay urgent and due regard to reports of slavery and forced labor. Nor has the government taken any legislative or administrative steps to regulate child labor performed in households or herding animals, nor has it ratified the ILO Minimum Age Convention.

Military Recruitment for the National Service of Underage Boys and Violation of their Freedom of Religion and that of Captured Young SPLA Soldiers

Underage children have been drafted as soldiers and into government-sponsored tribal militias, in violation of the Convention on the Rights of the Child and of Sudanese law, which provides that only men eighteen years of age and older may be conscripted.[1] The right of non-Muslim child conscripts to freedom of conscience and religion is violated during the training period when military trainers instruct and train them as "holy warriors" and refer to the conflict as an Islamic "holy war" against the south. The way in which religious studies are introduced in training recruits subjects the young conscripts to coercion that would impair their freedom to have a religion of their own choice. Nor are the non-Muslim recruits given an equal opportunity to manifest or practice their religion on the same basis as the Muslim conscripts.

In early 1995 there was widespread military conscription of young men involving a range of abuses, including the drafting of underage boys. Army officials, helped by members of the government's paramilitary Popular Defense Forces, set up checkpoints throughout the Khartoum area, and among others rounded up children as young as twelve. The street children's camps became a convenient reservoir from which to draw army conscripts. Recruitment efforts were not limited to the north. The army also forcibly drafted southerners in garrison towns to fight against their fellow southerners in the SPLA.

In 1992 the government of Sudan captured nineteen young SPLA soldiers who were too sick to be evacuated from Pochalla when it fell to the government. It took them to Khartoum for a brutal regime of forced Islamization, failing to respect the freedom of religion of these children.

---

[1] Human Rights Watch supports the adoption of the Protocol to the Convention on the Rights of the Child that would raise the minimum age of conscription to eighteen. Currently the international law standard is fifteen years.

Southern Sudan

The SPLA has long had a policy of separating boys from their homes and families for military training (and some education). Thousands of boys went to the Ethiopian refugee camps hoping for an education and received mostly military training. The SPLA inducted boys as young as eleven into its ranks.[2] With the sudden return of Sudanese refugees to Sudan when the Ethiopian government fell in May 1991, thousands of boys, who had been separated from their families but were not yet incorporated into the SPLA, arrived in southern Sudan. In 1993 UNICEF began a project to reunify willing boys with their willing families. This received the partial cooperation of the SPLA faction commanded by Riek Machar Terry Dhurgon, now called the Southern Sudan Independence Movement/Army (SSIM/A).

The SPLA never cooperated with UNICEF's family reunification program, preferring to keep the boys together under their thumb close to SPLA military facilities, and to call them up when needed. Thus boys in "unaccompanied minors" schools in Eastern Equatoria were called up in 1994 and 1995, as the SPLA continued to recruit minors. The SPLA denies child recruitment.

Although the SSIA cooperated with the UNICEF family reunification effort, unfortunately the faction did not stop underage recruitment. They lured hundreds of boys from their homes in Upper Nile to go hundreds of kilometers south to Eastern Equatoria, on the pretext that they would get schooling there. Instead they received military training at the base of Cmdr. William Nyuon, then a commander in the SSIA.

The boys received little food and no medical attention, however. As their condition worsened Cmdr. Nyuon sent them to the nearest U.N. relief site, Lafon, for medical aid and food; forty-seven boys died from malnutrition and illness in Lafon from July to December 1994. Among other things, SSIA soldiers stole their food rations. Subsequently the SSIA cooperated in a UNICEF family reunification program that airlifted hundreds of boys from Lafon back to their homes in Upper Nile.

Recommendations to the Government of Sudan:

- continue with the family reunification program for street children held in camps;

- proceed to a total phase-out of the camps by stopping "collection" and random capture of children from the streets, reunifying with their families children presently in the camps, and assuming responsibility for homeless

---

[2] *See* Human Rights Watch/Africa, Children's Rights Project, "Sudan: The Lost Boys: Child Soldiers and Unaccompanied Boys in Southern Sudan," *A Human Rights Watch Short Report*, vol. 6, no. 10 (November 1994).

- children and those whose families could not be traced through an adequate and acceptable welfare program which respects freedom of religion;

- investigate the allegations of ill-treatment of street children in the camps and punish those responsible;

- stop detaining street children unless they are suspected of committing a crime under the juvenile code and then are tried promptly with full due process rights, including notice to their families; alternatives to incarceration should be provided where feasible;

- continue to seek other, less drastic remedies for the problems of street children, that are consistent with the Convention on the Rights of the Child;

- ratify the African Convention on the Rights of the Child;

- take steps to put an immediate end to the abuse and capture of children during army and militia raids and their subsequent use as forced child labor in slavery-like conditions, including ordering a halt to the capture or arbitrary detention of children and other civilians in war zones;

- investigate and prosecute all reports of the kidnaping of civilians, especially children, in particular where this occurs during military actions carried out by governmental forces or their allies;

- investigate all reports of children held as servants or laborers, paid or unpaid, and all reports of physical or sexual abuse of these children, and prosecute those found responsible;

- investigate and prosecute officials and police officers who fail to enforce the criminal laws regarding child abuse, kidnaping, slavery, or forced or child labor, and consider increasing the penalties for those convicted of such failures to perform their duties;

- publicize such investigations and prosecutions as a means of deterrence;

- pass legislation outlawing unpaid employment of non-family members of whatever age;

- ratify the ILO Minimum Age Convention of 1973 (No. 138);

Summary and Recommendations 7

- prevent transportation by adults of unrelated children from state to state without appropriate authorization. Where the adult is of a different ethnic background from the child, the circumstances of such transport should be closely scrutinized;

- cooperate fully with the U.N. Committee on the Rights of the Child, the ILO, UNICEF, the U.N. Working Group on Contemporary Forms of Slavery, and the U.N. Commission on Human Rights' Special Rapporteur on Sudan in their investigations of the reported slavery-like abuses;

- request international cooperation, particularly technical assistance and advice, to pay urgent and due regard to reports of slavery and forced labor;

- refrain from using children under the age of eighteen as combatants, as that minimum age is provided for in Sudanese law, or in any capacity in military or militia structures, and prevent them from participating in such activities;

- respect the freedom of conscience and religion of all military conscripts or volunteers by exempting all those who wish to be exempted from religious studies and religiously-oriented military exercises, slogans, and activities; and

- provide safe land and air access for the provision of humanitarian aid to the children of Sudan throughout the national territory and without regard to who currently controls the territory.

Recommendations to the SPLM/A and SSIM/A:
- facilitate voluntary family reunification;

- cease all recruitment of children under the age of eighteen, including recruitment disguised as education;

- refrain from using children under the age of eighteen as combatants or in any capacity in military or militia structures, and prevent them from participating in such activities.

Recommendations to UNICEF, the ILO, the UNHCR, and others:

- UNICEF and the ILO should establish and fund programs to effectively promote the adoption of national legislation and implementing programs to ban child labor and slavery.

- Human Rights Watch recommends that UNICEF, the U.N. Committee on the Rights of the Child, the Working Group on Contemporary Forms of Slavery, the U.N. Commission on Human Rights' Special Rapporteur on Sudan, and the ILO monitor the application of the slavery and forced labor conventions to Sudan, and that all send fact-finding missions to investigate the reported abuses and the mechanisms the government is employing to confront the problem.

- conduct voluntary family reunification; where small groups of minors are separated from the larger tribe, efforts should be made to reunite them in the safest location, even if that means reuniting them outside Sudan or from one country of refuge to another.

Recommendation to the U.S., members of the European Union, and other concerned countries:

- pressure all parties to the conflict to improve their human rights performance by: 1) ceasing to use children under age eighteen as combatants or in any capacity in military or militia structures, and preventing them from participating in the conflict; 2) facilitating relief access and voluntary family reunification; and 3) supporting measures in international forums and in Sudan to effectively end child labor and slavery.

PART I

ABUSES BY THE GOVERNMENT OF SUDAN

2
STREET CHILDREN

The Applicable Law
  Due Process

The Sudan government has had a program of capturing children from city streets and sending them to closed street children's camps. It has conducted this program for the most part without any effort to identify the child's family, its whereabouts, and if the child is living with his family. The result has been that many children, who left home only to run an errand, have been held for years in these closed camps, while their families frantically have searched for them.

The government separates the alleged "street children" from their families without notice or any judicial oversight. The children are placed in camps run by the state, for indeterminate periods that last years, without recourse to any legislation such as the Juvenile Welfare Act of 1983.[3] The Juvenile Care Council (JCC) is the state agency, under the state welfare ministries, that runs these camps. This entire process grossly violates the Convention on the Rights of the Child,[4] which provides in Article 9 (1) that:

> States Parties shall ensure that a child shall not be separated from his or her parents against their will, except when competent authorities subject to judicial review determine, in accordance with applicable law and procedures, that such separation is necessary for the best interest of the child. . . .

---

[3] *See* U.N. Economic and Social Council, Commission on Human Rights, Fiftieth Session, "Situation of human rights in the Sudan, report of Special Rapporteur, Mr. Gáspár Biró," E/CN.4/1994/48 (Geneva: United Nations, February 1, 1994) ("Special Rapporteur Biró, Report of February 1994"), p. 28.

[4] Sudan became a party to this convention on August 3, 1990. It was among the early ratifiers of the convention, and ratified without reservations. It was obliged to submit a report to the Committee on the Rights of the Child on September 1, 1992, which it did on September 29, 1992, and after its submission the committee requested substantial additional information. The full text of the Convention on the Rights of the Child is in the Appendix.

The African Charter also protects the child within the family unit.[5]

The U.N. Human Rights Commission's Special Rapporteur has identified this as "a case of arbitrary arrest and detention without due process of law."[6] We agree.

In the case of boys, the state does not make any effort to identify the parents or relatives, according to the boys.[7] Government authorities from police to camp administrators simply do not ask for information about relatives, and, what is worse, reject it if it is offered. Even a street children's camp employee of Dawa Islamiya, whom the guards selected for us to interview, was originally summarily interned in a camp although he told the police he had a job and lived with his aunt. This boy, now age eighteen, is a Muslim from the Nuba Mountains. A summary of his testimony follows:

> Three years ago, in May 1992 when he was fifteen, he was picked up by the police when he was out on the street after work. The police accused him of being a vagrant. He believes this was because he was wearing dirty clothes. He told the police that he had a family and a job, "But they did not listen to me," he said. He had a job as a ticket collector on the buses in Khartoum. His family lived in Jebel Aulia, an official displaced persons camp some forty kilometers south of Khartoum, and he stayed with his aunt in Khartoum.
>
> They sent him to the camp at El Fau where he remained until June 1993 when that camp was "finished," or closed and its boys sent to Soba. He did not have any contact with his family at all when he was in El Fau, and they had no idea what had happened to him.[8]

---

[5] The African Charter, Art. 18, states: "1. The family shall be the natural unit and basis of society. It shall be protected by the State which shall take care of its physical and moral health. 2. The State shall have the duty to assist the family which is the custodian of morals and traditional values recognized by the community.

[6] Special Rapporteur Biró, Report of February 1994, p. 28.

[7] Ibid.

[8] Now that he is employed at Soba, he sees them on Thursday and Friday. Interview, Khartoum, May 9, 1995.

It appears that this one-way street to the closed camp is so well known in the poor communities from which the "street children" are plucked that some boys give false names, intending to escape.

In the sole facility for girls, the Dar Bacha'er Home for Girls, the parents were sometimes contacted but even then they and the girls had few rights. Parents and girls are subjected to arbitrary procedures in which there is no opportunity for the courts to check the whims of any camp administrator. The JCC admitted that no court has jurisdiction over the camp or how the girls arrive at and are held in the home: "The court had nothing to do with them."[9] Thus, even after the pilot family reunification program was conducted at Dar Bacha'er, the home was no model of due process.

A JCC official explained that after 1 a.m. nightly, the Public Order Police *(an nizam al amm)* tour the city. These police who bring in the girls are not the regular police; they belong to a special branch of the police that "takes care of beggars, street children, thieves, crazy people." If they find girls on the street, in houses of prostitution, or with alcohol, they bring them to this facility.

They affirmed that the staff investigates the family background of the girls. If the family wants the girl back and the officials disagree, then it is the practice to require a male relative to submit a written guarantee that he will take care of the girl. The mother may also take responsibility for the girl, they added when questioned. It was clear during our interview of the gathered staff members that the procedures are extremely loose and arbitrary. It is unclear which agency has ultimate authority, if any does. Apparently the more assertive families go to the police and the JCC and ask them to write letters authorizing the release of the girl. Either these agencies or the camp authorities may require a guarantee from a relative.

If the girl is found on the street a second time, the camp will not release her again and she will be kept there for two years, all without any judicial proceedings. Other staff members verified that they have never had to go to court to get a judge's approval to remove a girl from her family: "The courts do not interfere." One social work assistant who had worked at the home for three years said there were perhaps forty such cases of girls who returned to the street after such an undertaking.

Asked whether there had ever been any case of disagreement between the authorities and a girl's family, two of the social work assistants said that if the family feels strongly about it, they would give the girl back. "There is no specific law on this."

Since due process is lacking even where the parents are contacted, mere parental notification will not suffice. The camps must be closed.

---

[9] Interview, Abdullah Hassan, Dar Bacha'er Home for Girls, Omdurman, May 9, 1995.

Religious Freedom

No governmental official to whom we spoke officially defends violation of the religious freedom of the children, nor insists that the state has the right to convert children from their own religion to Islam. Officials simply deny that such violations exist.

The efforts to force children in these camps to convert and to practice Islam are well documented and pervasive, however. Our investigations confirmed what others have found.[10] Here also, the practice is simply not to ask the child if he has a religion and what it is, but to treat him as a Muslim or a clean slate on which to imprint a religion. One government official asked us what was wrong with teaching Islam to children. When we pointed out that if the child already had another religion, this could be a violation of religious freedom, the official had no answer. [11]

We do not doubt that many state officials genuinely feel they are acting in the best interests of the child by giving him or her a religious Islamic education. Nevertheless, in probably the majority of cases, they are violating the Convention on the Rights of the Child, Article 14:

> 1. States Parties shall respect the right of the child to freedom of thought, conscience and religion.
> 2. States Parties shall respect the rights and duties of the parents and, when applicable, legal guardians, to provide direction to the child in the exercise of his or her right in a manner consistent with the evolving capacities of the child.

---

[10]*See*, Human Rights Watch/Africa, "In the Name of God: Repression Continues in Northern Sudan," *A Human Rights Watch Short Report*, vol. 6, no. 9 (November 1994), pp. 20-23. Others who have reported on this situation include Special Rapporteur Biró, Report of February 1994, pp. 26-33; U.N. Economic and Social Council, Commission on Human Rights, Fifty-first session, "Situation of human rights in the Sudan, Report of the Special Rapporteur, Mr. Gáspár Biró," E/CN.4/1995/58 (Geneva: United Nations, January 30, 1995) ("Special Rapporteur Biró, Report of January 1995"), pp. 7-11; Amnesty International, *The Tears of Orphans: No Future without human rights* (London: Amnesty International Publications, January 1995), pp. 41-42; Statement of Dr. Kevin Vigilante, MD, representative of the Puebla Institute, before the Subcommittee on Africa of the Committee on International Relations, U.S. House of Representatives (March 22, 1995); African Rights, *Sudan's Invisible Citizens: The Policy of Abuse Against Displaced People in the North* (London: African Rights, March 1995), pp. 17-20; African Rights, *Facing Genocide: The Nuba of Sudan* (London: African Rights, July 1995), pp. 257-58.

[11]Interview, Ghazi Salah al Din, State Minister of Foreign Affairs, Khartoum, May 4, 1995.

> 3. Freedom to manifest one's religion or beliefs may be subject only to such limitations as are prescribed by law and are necessary to protect public safety, order, health, or morals or the fundamental rights and freedoms of others.

They are also violating the religious freedom provisions of the African Charter[12] and the International Covenant on Civil and Political Rights.[13]

At Dar Bacha'er Home for girls, the staff admitted that they did not ask the religion of the girls during the intake process or afterwards. When asked how they knew the girls' religion, they said that, as to the Christian girls, the staff "heard them singing church songs."

The staff denied that they gave any religious instruction to the girls.

This was flatly contradicted by the girls we interviewed privately. One thirteen-year-old girl whom the staff chose for us to interview had participated in the family reunification program and had returned for the day to visit. She had been in the home for more than two years. According to her, the daily routine included Islamic prayers five times a day, in which everyone participated, even the southern and Christian girls. First they got up and prayed in the mosque, cleaned the room, queued up and went to school, prayed, had lunch, rested, and prayed at sunset.

In the afternoon they sometimes played sports and prayed beforehand. In the evening they had Koran readings and study in which all girls participated. They would watch television and have evening prayers before they went to bed.

Her family, from the Nuba Mountains, is Muslim but some girls in the camp are Christian and they still had to join in the same prayers, she said. An eight-year-old girl said that at school all girls study the same subjects: religion (the Koran), Arabic, and math.

The religious regime for the boys was similar.

---

[12] The African Charter, Art. 8, provides: "Freedom of conscience, the profession and free practice of religion shall be guaranteed. No one may, subject to law and order, be submitted to measures restricting the exercise of these freedoms."

[13] The International Covenant on Civil and Political Rights, Art. 18, provides: "1. Everyone shall have the right to freedom of thought, conscience and religion. This right shall include freedom to have or to adopt a religion or belief of his choice, and freedom, either individually or in community with others and in public, or private, to manifest his religion or belief in worship, observance, practice and teaching. . . . 4. The States Parties to the present Covenant undertake to have respect for the liberty of parents and, when applicable, legal guardians to ensure the religious and moral education of their children in conformity with their own convictions."

Right to Preserve Identity

Many children are given new names in Arabic to replace their Christian or southern tribal names that often identify the place of origin or tribe of the child. This violates the right of the child, protected by the Convention on the Rights of the Child, "to preserve his or her identity, including nationality, name and family relations as recognized by law without unlawful interference."[14]

The Convention on the Rights of the Child recognizes that a child temporarily deprived of his or her family environment shall be entitled to special protection and assistance provided by the state. This could include *Kafala*[15] of Islamic law, but all protection and assistance must be given with "due regard . . . paid to the child's ethnic, religious, cultural and linguistic background."[16]

There is no regard whatsoever paid to the child's ethnic, religious, cultural or linguistic background in the camps for street children; as far as we can determine, there is not even any inquiry made into these subjects. On the contrary, it appears that the staff makes an effort to avoid knowing anything about the child's prior identity. They simply treat all children as Muslims and Arabs, although the majority of the children are southerners and were neither Muslims nor Arabs before they were summarily interned in the camps.[17]

This was clearest in the case of one confused eight-year-old we interviewed at the Soba camp for street boys, whose testimony is summarized below.

---

[14] Convention on the Rights of the Child, Art. 8 (1).

[15] *Kafala* is sponsorship of orphans paid for by individuals as part of their religious duty. The government in its statement to the Committee on the Rights of the Child in 1993 described the *kafala* system as "similar to adoption and [which] ensured that children were placed within the extended family rather than with a family with which they had no ties." U.N., Convention on the Rights of the Child, Committee on the Rights of the Child, Fourth session, Summary Record of the 90th Meeting, held 29 September 1993, CRC/C/SR.90 (Geneva: 5 October 1993), p. 5.

[16] Convention on the Rights of the Child, Art. 20 (3). *See Ibid.*, Art. 30 (protection of minorities).

[17] This finding also reinforces similar findings by other investigators. *See* footnote 10, above.

This small boy had an Arabic name, Mahmoud (not his real Arabic name).[18] Since he looked southern, we asked his father's name. It was John (a Christian name). His mother's name was Rosa (not a Muslim name). Mahmoud said he himself had another name when he was young and living with his family, but he does not remember it. The authorities gave him the name Mahmoud when they took him to the first boys' camp.

He told us his tribe was Dinka; his mother is Dinka and his father is from the Nuba Mountains. His mother is a Muslim and his father a Christian, he said.[19]

When they captured him, he was about six years old. He was living with his family in Port Sudan; he has one brother and one sister. His father sent him to get food from the market. The police caught him en route to the market and he never saw his family again. They took him to El Fau camp and later to Soba camp.

We asked if he told the police that he had a family. He spoke softly: "They did not give me a chance to speak. The police put me in the car and took me to the camp."

No one ever asked him where he came from, where his parents were, what were their names, and what, if anything, was their religion.

Background

In 1987, during the democratically-elected government, several different NGOs undertook projects to address the problem of street children. They included Amal (Hope), Sabah (Morning), Sudan Popular Committee for Relief and Rehabilitation, St. Vincent De Paul (which worked with southern children in Khartoum), and the African Society for Mother and Child Care, a subgroup of Dawa Islamiya (Islamic Call, a large Islamic NGO that works in more than fifteen African countries).

---

[18] The names that have been changed in this report are on file with Human Rights Watch.

[19] Orthodox Islam denies non-Muslim men the right to marry a Muslim woman. A Muslim man may marry a woman of any religion. Nevertheless, this is what the boy said about his parents.

A pamphlet issued by the Sudanese Juvenile Care Organization[20] in 1989 spells out some ideological reasons driving Islamists' interest in street children: it explains that child vagrancy has led to the "domination of the left over street children, since it exploits them in sabotage by talking to them about class differences."

After the 1989 military coup and takeover of government power by the National Islamic Front, an Islamist political party that ran a poor third in 1986 national elections, the rules of the game were changed. The Ministry of Social Welfare in 1991 instituted strict new regulations, purportedly on quality control grounds, that had the effect of prohibiting all NGOs from running residency programs for street children. It made other programs targeted at street children by non-Islamic NGOs very difficult, until the recent family reunification pilot project in which UNICEF and two international NGOs took an important role.

Beginning in September 1992, Khartoum State authorities undertook to "cleanse" the city of street children, considered a threat to public order and a blight on the capital. Police and city authorities began routinely rounding up vagrant children by night from places where they slept, such as in the markets, and taking them to camps outside the capital and in other states.

In its submission to the U.N. Committee on the Rights of the Child in 1993, the Sudan government said that there were 23,931 homeless children in Sudan (64.97 percent of them "partly" homeless). It said that three major foster and family rehabilitation centers in Khartoum, Kosti (Central Province), and Geneina (Darfur) were "ready to take in homeless, orphaned and other similar groups of children."The Home of the Future (Dar Bacha'er) for girls was ready to take up to 300 girls.[21]

The street children camps are now under the jurisdiction of the federal Ministry of Social Planning and the state welfare authorities. The Juvenile Care Council, which in Khartoum is an agency under the Minister of Social Welfare for Khartoum State, administers them.[22] Food in at least some camps is provided by the

---

[20] This nonprofit organization is considered to be the predecessor of the Juvenile Care Council (JCC).

[21] U.N. Convention on the Rights of the Child, Committee on the Rights of the Child, Initial reports of States parties due in 1992: Sudan dated September 29, 1992, CRC/C/3/Add.3 (Geneva: December 1992) p. 17.

[22] Interview, Abdullah Hassan, Dar Bacha'er Home for Girls, Omdurman, May 9, 1995.

international nongovernmental organization Adventist Development and Relief Agency (ADRA) and *zakat*[23] provides resources also.

The JCC consists of representatives of the Ministry of Social Welfare, the Zakat Chamber and nongovernment organizations. The director of Social Welfare for Khartoum State was the General Secretary of the JCC for more than two years, followed by one and a half years in his current post.[24]

Only St. Vincent de Paul of all NGOs now continues a residency program for street children; officially its program was dissolved in 1994 but it was permitted to continue these activities because there was no other place to place the 150 southern children it was feeding, housing and educating in some seven homes in Khartoum. Its administrator, who was also the director of a breakfast program for more than eighty schools in slum areas in greater Khartoum, was arrested in April 1994 and held for ten days with three Egyptian seminarists, volunteers in the breakfast program, who were suspected of espionage. None was charged with a crime. Sudan Security withheld the vehicle in which they were arrested, which reportedly was carrying a large amount of money in cash, apparently the salaries of teachers in the schools covered by the program. The money and the vehicle were not returned, and the administrator filed a complaint in November to recuperate both. It was in reprisal for this action that he was apparently beaten by a security agent from Sudan Security's department of church activities (*an shitta al kanasiya*) in charge of the case. Ultimately the Commissioner of Voluntary Agencies (COVA), the Ministry of Social Planning agency with jurisdiction over national and international NGOs, suspended the registration of Saint Vincent de Paul.

The years-old practice of seizing children from the street, without notice to their parents, has led to a subculture of relatives and others who search for missing

---

[23] Zakat is a religious tax on excess money (such as liquid assets in savings, livestock and agricultural production), presently collected by the Zakat Chamber, a federal body under the Ministry of Social Planning charged with collecting and distributing zakat. According to the teachings of Islam, zakat must be distributed to eight categories: the destitute, debtors with no means of repaying their debt, travelers with no lodgings, to free those enslaved, those who are inclined to Islam but not yet converted, jihad, and salaries for those administering zakat. In principle, the Zakat Chamber should distribute all money collected within the year of collection. Street children would fall into the category of the destitute.

[24] Interview, Mumdi Mohammed Salah, Director, Social Welfare of Khartoum State, Khartoum, June 10, 1995.

children and advise and help each other.[25] Their efforts are not always successful, or are successful only after crucial years in a young child's life have been spent in harsh camp conditions, deprived of all contact with his or her family. The testimony of one father is summarized below.[26]

> Marial (not his real name) migrated to Khartoum with his family in 1983, before the war in the south was "serious." He is a Dinka from Rumbek, and a Christian. In about 1990, when his son, Michael (not his real name), was about ten or eleven, Marial sent Michael to the market in Omdurman to run an errand. The son disappeared. Marial did not find his son for three years. He finally found Michael in a camp for street boys perhaps fifty kilometers north of Khartoum, which may have been Abu Doum, although Marial, who is illiterate, did not remember the name of the camp. His story is typical of the efforts to which parents go to find their "street" children; his story, unlike many others, had a happy ending.
>
> Here, the father was helped by the fact that there were many southern parents in the Khartoum area searching for their disappeared or kidnaped children, although without any help from the authorities. One group of searchers found this camp one morning's drive by car north of Khartoum. In this camp there were at least 150 children, all boys.
>
> The searchers managed to talk privately to some of the "black-looking boys." The adults, who were from Omdurman, asked where the boys came from. Marial's son Michael volunteered his real name as well as the false name he had given to the authorities [some boys give false names, hoping to escape], and said he too was from Omdurman.

---

[25] Searches are not just for street children taken from the streets to camps by officials; people whose children have been abducted during military raids in war zones also spend years trying to find their children, many of whom have ended up in conditions of slavery as unpaid domestic servants. Families whose boys have been conscripted without notice also search for their sons. *See* below.

[26] Interview, Khartoum, May 21, 1995.

Another Rumbek parent whose son also was taken to a camp helped Marial. This man told Marial where to go to get the papers necessary to free his son from the camp. Those who operated the camp are "an Islamic group that has an office in Khartoum," but the father forgets the name. He gathered documents from this and a variety of other offices.

When Marial arrived at the camp, his son recognized him and ran to him, with another boy, a relative. His son told him that when he was captured at the Omdurman market the police just threw him into a car. They did not ask any questions or give him a chance to say who he was and where his parents were. When finally asked his name, he gave them a false one.

When Marial presented the documents to the camp officials, they at first refused to release the boy. Marial insisted that he wanted his son back so he could send him to school. The camp officials told him they took his son and the other children because "the way that they were living in town was degrading to Sudan, bad for foreigners to see them living in garbage." They had to take the boys out of town. In the camp, the officials said, the children were living better than in the streets. They were in a proper place, and had people taking care of them.

These officials finally released the son, however. In all the son spent three years, from age ten to thirteen, illegally separated from his family.

Facilities
Abu Doum Camp for Boys

Currently the largest facility for street children is the Abu Doum camp north of Omdurman, where as of June 1995 about 650 boys lived, according to the Director of Social Welfare of Khartoum State. It has housed up to 1,000 boys.[27] Reportedly some 200-300 boys were picked up from the streets of Khartoum around December

---

[27] Interview, Mumdi M. Salih, Director, Social Welfare of Khartoum State, Khartoum, June 10, 1995.

1994 and taken there. This was the last large roundup as of May 1995, although such roundups have been conducted periodically ever since the program began in 1992.[28]

The Abu Doum camp is close to a military base and military checkpoints, making access without a government guide impossible. Because the road is very bad, it takes about two hours in an all-terrain vehicle to reach the camp from Khartoum, according to state authorities. The vast majority of the boys in this camp, according to people who have visited, are originally from the south and west of Sudan, although they were picked up mostly in Khartoum.

The authorities justify the inconvenient location of this camp on the grounds that it removes the boys from the bad influences in Khartoum, where they could leave rehabilitation homes and purchase and inhale benzene and engage in other undesirable activities. In addition, the authorities admit that boys escaped from these Khartoum homes.

While Ministry of Social Planning officials say that the Abu Doum boys go to elementary school in the local village, visit their families, and receive visits from their families, we were not able to verify this.[29] Other human rights monitors have reported that the families of the boys do not visit them since the families are not informed that the children were placed in the camp in the first place.

In the case of Marial, referred to above, Marial made a few observations about the camp where he found his son (which was probably Abu Doum Camp):

> Marial noticed that the boys in the camp were all ages: younger and older than his son, to judge by their heights. All the boys in this camp were "black," he said.

---

[28] Interview, Khartoum, May 3, 1995. In its submission to the Committee on the Rights of the Child in June 1993, the government said that there were 480 boys at Hajar Abu Dum, located in the rural north of Khartoum Province. It stated the camp was for boys seven through nine, U.N., Convention on the Rights of the Child, Committee on the Rights of the Child, "Initial reports of States parties due in 1992, Addendum, Sudan, 2 June 1993," CRC/C/3/Add.20 (Geneva: 2 August 1993) ("Sudan Submission of June 1993 to CRC"), p. 9. This was contradicted by those who visited the camp, including the U.N. Commission on Human Rights' Special Rapporteur on Sudan, Gáspár Biró. Special Rapporteur Biró, Report of February 1994, p. 29.

[29] Human Rights Watch's planned visit to Abu Doum did not take place because the director of the institution failed to arrive at the designated time for departure, and because of illness. The visit was postponed until the next Human Rights Watch mission to Sudan. The camp was visited by Special Rapporteur Gáspár Biró, however. *See* Special Rapporteur Biró, Report of February 1994, p. 29.

In the camp, according to his son, they were taught how to weave with their hands and feet, producing a *tagiya* or skullcap. They did not wear this skullcap.

His son also told him that their Islamic training consisted of prayers starting at 4 a.m., and going on from there for the required five prayers a day. There were no Christian prayers or services in the camp, no church, and no priests or ministers visiting. All boys were required to participate in Islamic rites, whatever their religion. The son told him that he had not received military training, however.

Marial observed a big fence all around the camp. Inside this compound were small huts with thatched roofs (papyrus), no zinc, no bricks. He saw where the boys slept: the accommodations were "all right." There were eight to ten beds in each room.

The boys, however, were constantly running away. Some escaped but others were caught. His son did not try to escape because he was "too young."

The camp officials used to lash the boys, and would make some boys lash the others. All the boys were thin and looked fragile, he assumed because of the beatings; their health did not look good. His son knew one boy who died in the camp; he was ill and the authorities tried to give him medical treatment but he died anyway.[30]

Soba Camp for Boys

The Soba camp houses about eighty boys, ages seven through seventeen, according to the guards, who said it has a capacity for one hundred boys. We observed that the majority of boys were not yet adolescents and these young boys looked like southerners.

Although the Minister of Social Planning and Minister of Social Welfare for Khartoum State, which runs the camp through the JCC, told us that Soba was a

---

[30] Interview, Khartoum, May 21, 1995.

temporary reception home where boys stayed for seven to ten days on average,[31] the guards said that some boys had been there for two years, and many had been there for six or seven months. Soba was not listed as a homeless children's facility by the government in its submission in June 1993 to the U.N. Committee on the Rights of the Child.

The Soba camp was opened a few years ago, closed, then reopened two years ago, the guards said, apparently when camps in other states were closed due to funding problems. It is located close to the African Islamic University in Khartoum, tucked behind other social welfare institutes such as the African Center for Mother and Child Care run by Dawa Islamiya, and is not marked.

We visited the camp without a government escort because we had been told by the government before the mission started that we could move freely in Sudan without an escort, and visit anywhere we wanted. We hoped to receive more candid comments from camp officials and children if we visited without a prior appointment. There were only guards present when we visited Soba on May 9, 1995, but they consented to our visit and even to some private interviews with the boys before changing their minds.

The religious training was obvious upon our arrival at about 1:15 p.m.; they told us all the boys and staff were at their midday Islamic prayers. We had to wait while they finished. After a few minutes, they emerged from the prayer area. Many were young southern boys and some still had sand on their foreheads from where they had bowed down. When we spoke to a group of them apart from the guards, they said they were all required to say Islamic prayers five times a day. They identified themselves as from Dinka, Shilluk, Nuer, Azande, and other southern tribes, and said their families did not raise them as Muslims.

The guards told us that the boys, mostly from the south, were Muslim and Christian although the "great majority are Muslim," we were assured.

The Soba camp is not, like Abu Doum is and El Fau was, a closed camp. Indeed, its Khartoum location would make it hard to prevent boys from escaping. Some boys said that Soba was better than the El Fau camp because El Fau was a closed camp, and no one could go in or out. In El Fau, however, one added, the food was better than in Soba. Other boys said that staying at the Soba camp was preferable to being exposed to police harassment on the streets of Khartoum; most boys were very far from their families since their internment in these camps, and have no where else to go.

---

[31] Interview, Bedawi Haj Hassan, Minister of Social Planning, and Mumdi Mohammed Salih, Director of Social Welfare, Khartoum State, Khartoum, June 10, 1995.

Street Children 25

We privately interviewed two older boys (one a camp employee) the guards chose for us and two younger boys we chose. We began to interview a thirteen-year-old boy we had chosen, who identified himself as a member of a southern tribe from Juba. Three guards then entered the room and were very rude, insisting we had talked to enough boys. "One is enough. You are not writing a book. They all will say the same thing. We treat them all the same way. The boys do not remember well. Why do you want to talk to them in private? We know what you want to ask. [They did not spell this out.] The boys are frightened that they will be called to talk to you." The visit was terminated.

The remarks of the guards, however, suggested that they feared that the boys might talk about ill-treatment at this facility.

Testimonies from Soba

The testimonies of two boys we interviewed privately are summarized below:

Musa (not his real name), who gave his age as eight, said he was from the Tamawi tribe, from western Sudan. His family was living in Ombada in Omdurman, but the police caught him on the streets of Khartoum, where he was spending most of his time. This happened "a long time ago." He was first sent to a camp in Port Sudan (about 1,190 kilometers from Omdurman).[32] This camp was "very bad." Sometimes they did not get water, sometimes they did not get food. After a year in Port Sudan they moved him to the El Fau camp, where there was enough food at first. Then conditions in El Fau worsened and they moved him and the rest of the boys to Soba.

He told the police when they picked him up that he had a family, but they did not listen to him. He has not seen his parents or siblings since the police took him away. When he told us how many brothers and sisters he had, two sisters and five brothers, his eyes began to tear.

One fifteen-year-old boy, Hussein (not his real name), whom the guards selected to talk to us, was a runaway who now wants to go

---

[32] This camp may have been Durdib, described below. It was intended to prepare older boys to join the military.

home but cannot. At age twelve he left his home in Geneina, Darfur, near the Chadian border, because he did not want to go to school. He jumped a train in Nyalla, Darfur, and the police caught him on the train in Kosti. The police took him to the El Fau camp for a year and then they sent him to Soba two years ago, in 1993.

He emphasized that he would like to go home very much. He misses his parents. He has two brothers and three sisters also, but has had no contact at all with his family for three years. He does not have the money for the fare home, however. He was ashamed that he does not have any decent clothes, only two ragged shirts and pants.

We asked if he told the camp authorities that he wanted to return home; he had, but they said they did not have enough money for his fare. It came out later in the interview, however, that they did manage to transport him and fifty-four other boys from the Soba camp to El Muglad in mid-1994. There they presented the boys with the option of joining the army or returning to the Soba camp. They provided free military transport to and from El Muglad, which is quite a distance from Khartoum, about 1,050 kilometers.

Although he completed a metalworking course (making window grating and beds) and received a certificate,[33] he could find work only as a bus ticket collector in Khartoum in early 1995. Like so many young men, however, he was afraid of forced recruitment; his bus route passed inside Khartoum, where "the soldiers catch all the boys and put them in camps for training and take them to the south to fight." He had no identification to show his age, fifteen, three years below the official draft age, so he quit his job rather than risk the draft. He could not find other work to pay for his ticket home.

---

[33] The guards said that the Soba camp has a training program that lasts two years (construction skills), conducted outside the camp. The guards pointed to wall where several certificates of completion of the course were hung, each of which bore a boy's photograph. The eighteen-year-old employee of Dawa Islamiya at the camp also received a certificate after completing this two-year course.

Dar Bacha'er Home for Girls

The only camp for girls is Dar Bacha'er Home, in Omdurman, which is run by the JCC under the Minister of Social Welfare for Khartoum State. At the beginning of the pilot project in 1994 it had a population of fifty-six girls, mostly southerners. [34] The Ministry of Social Planning has reunified twenty-six girls with their families through the pilot program run with UNICEF and two NGOs; only fourteen girls remained in the home as of May 1995. The girls in the pilot program ranged from ages six to twelve and they had been in the home for an average of three to four years. [35]

This camp is the only one for girl street children in all of Sudan. It is for the three towns area: Khartoum, North Khartoum, and Omdurman. This home is not intended for girls facing juvenile criminal proceedings. If there is a criminal court case against them, the girls are not brought here. They take these girls, usually ages fourteen and older, directly to the women's prison in Omdurman.

As with the Soba camp, we visited Dar Bacha'er without prior appointment on May 9, 1995. We talked briefly to social work assistants until a representative of the JCC arrived. This man, Abdallah Hassan, turned out to be the director of the boys' camp at Abu Doum. [36]

He told us that the family reunification pilot project removed all the girls who were in the facility in 1994. The fourteen girls now there were rounded up after January 1995. [37] He admitted that the police continue to round up street girls and that it is the home's intention to keep them in the camp for two years. While claiming that the new girls are to be included in the reunification program, those interviewed described several steps that must first be taken: the girls are to receive health care, be taught a skill, and the families are to be contacted.

Education will take two years, the social work assistants and JCC representative estimated; at the time of our visit there seemed to be more staff than girls on the grounds. The girls usually do not go to the local school for academic education, although they are permitted to if they want. The thirteen-year-old girl to whom we spoke confirmed that she had completed second and third grades at a local

---

[34] In its submission to the Committee on the Rights of the Child in 1993, the government said that there were sixty-two children in this facility. Sudan Submission of June 1993 to CRC, p. 9.

[35] Interview, UNICEF, May 3, 1995.

[36] He was introduced to us in this capacity by the Minister of Social Welfare of Khartoum State a month later.

[37] The discrepancy in the numbers was not explained.

school and is now in fourth grade. Most girls receive vocational skills education, including handicrafts, such as embroidering burlap curtains. They also teach them moral values.

While sometimes the facility receives no new girls for weeks, the most recently arrived girls were brought in by the police one week before our visit to Dar Bacha'er. The three girls were picked up in one group. They released two of them to their families but they had not notified the family of the third, for an unknown reason.

Of the three, one ten or eleven-year-old was deaf, according to a social work assistant. First they kept her for three days "to make sure that she was not just pretending to be deaf. " Once they were convinced she was not pretending, they put her in a car and she pointed out her house for them and was left there. She came from a Dinka family living outside Omdurman.

The second girl told them her address. She stayed five days, then her mother came to pick her up. She too was from a Dinka family.

The third girl, a small child, very timid, who told us she was eight, said her family is from Tama in Darfur. She has one brother and eight sisters who live in Dar Es Salaam displaced persons camp in Omdurman. Her mother does not know where she is, she said.

Other camps

There was a boys' camp in El Fau, between Wad Medani and Gedaref, but that camp is now abandoned, as investigators discovered in 1995.[38] In its submission to the U.N. Committee on the Rights of the Child in June 1993, the government said

---

[38] Dr. Kevin Vigilante visited an empty camp at Fau II on February 1, 1995 and interviewed the police guards, who told him the camp had about 230 children but they had been taken to another camp at Soba on September 9, 1994. He also visited an empty camp at Wad Medani for vocational training. Statement of Dr. Kevin Vigilante, MD, representative of the Puebla Institute, before the Subcommittee on Africa of the Committee on International Relations, U.S. House of Representatives, March 22, 1995, p. 3.

Another nongovernmental investigator visiting on July 13, 1994, who wishes to remain anonymous, found that there were 457 youth at the camp at the time; they had no contact with their families, according to a policeman at the camp. The camp was called Farouq 2 at Fau 2, about thirty-two kilometers from El Fau. That camp director told the investigator that administrative reorganization required the state instead of the federal government to provide for the feeding of the children, which it had not done; the boys were being fed (poorly) with food provided by local merchants on loans.

The boys we interviewed placed the closure of the El Fau camp at an earlier date; there may have been more than one camp in the El Fau area.

this camp had 460 boys and was intended for boys between the ages of ten and thirteen.[39]

At Soba camp we interviewed boys who spent one or two years in El Fau camp which, we were told by a knowledgeable source, was disbanded because the administration of the newly created state refused to fund the program. (In early 1994 Sudan underwent yet another administrative reorganization and twenty-six states were created where there had been nine.) The new state decided the camp was too costly. Furthermore, the boys in El Fau camp were strangers to the state, having been brought from Khartoum or other cities. They were relocated to the Soba camp in Khartoum.

A camp in Durdib in the Red Sea Hills of eastern Sudan, not far from Port Sudan, also was used for street children; according to the government, in June 1993 it housed 278 boys in a permanent building.[40] It now appears to be used solely for adult military training purposes.[41]

In Juba, the largest southern town and former regional capital, the interned street children population is said to consist mostly of boys from Kajo Keiji near the Ugandan border. The war displaced them with their families to the Juba neighborhood of Kuku.[42]

The government admitted to four camps in June 1993: Abu Doum, El Fau, Durdib, and Dar Bacha'er. Obviously Soba and the camp in Juba have been added, while El Fau and Durdib have been closed. Other nongovernment investigations have discovered several other camps for street children arbitrarily arrested and detained without due process in these camps by the state;[43] our investigation of this matter is not complete and we know of no definitive list of current street children's camps.

---

[39] Sudan Submission of June 1993 to CRC, pp. 9-10.

[40] Ibid. It was intended for boys between the ages of fourteen and eighteen.

[41] A nongovernmental researcher who wishes to remain anonymous visited the Durdib camp on July 7, 1994, and found it vacant. The police guarding the camp said that it was opened in 1992 and graduated two classes of youth (one class of 775 and another of 685) from harsh military and religious training. Food, clothing, and housing were very bad and many children fell ill; many others tried to escape. Punishment was harsh, all according to the police.

The information that it is currently being used for adult military training was provided in May 1995.

[42] Interview, UNICEF, May 3, 1995.

[43] African Rights, "Sudan's Invisible Citizens," pp. 17-18, lists seven camps.

Recent Improvements

This deplorable state of affairs may be partially remedied by a Ministry of Social Planning family reunification program with support of UNICEF, Oxfam/UK and Radda Barnen.[44] They conducted the pilot project for this program with street girls at the Dar Bacha'er Home. It appears that the government permitted this project in part because of the human rights furor that arose over the above-mentioned abuses.[45] In addition, camps are not cost effective: they absorb resources and actually reach very few children. The results of this pilot project were favorable. The government of Sudan has said it will permit a family reunification project for the hundreds of boys held in the boys' camp at Abu Doum to begin as early as August 1995.[46] It will be necessary to monitor the progress of this effort.

---

[44]Oxfam/UK assisted in developing an income-generating project for the impoverished families of the street girls.

[45]*See* Special Rapporteur Biró, Report of February 1994.

[46]Interview with Bedawi Haj Hassan, Minister of Social Planning, and Mumdi Mohammed Salih, Social Welfare, Khartoum State, June 10, 1995, Khartoum.

3
SLAVERY OR FORCED LABOR OF MINORS KIDNAPED FROM THEIR FAMILIES DURING MILITIA RAIDS

The practices described as slavery in Sudan have their current origin in the human rights abuses committed in the civil war by government troops and militia in the south and the Nuba Mountains. These abuses did not start with the current government which took power in June 1989. They routinely were committed by Arab militias armed by local government and the Umma Party under the democratically-elected government (1986-89) of Prime Minister and Umma Party president Sadiq al-Mahdi.

Arab militias, which have under the current government been loosely incorporated into the Popular Defense Forces (PDF),[47] were armed for the purpose of defeating the rebel SPLA by attacking its alleged social base in southern Kordofan and northern Bahr El Ghazal, within raiding distance of the Arab raiders. The targets were principally the Nuba and Dinka peoples which to some extent were traditional rivals of the Arab tribes. In addition to being effectively licensed by state and federal governments to attack these civilians with impunity, the Arab militias were permitted to loot cattle, burn property, and take civilians captive. Army soldiers and officers as well as militia have captured and kept civilians as personal household slaves.

These civilians, mostly women and children, were not captured for the purpose of criminal prosecution by the authorities. Nor were they captured as hostages in tribal negotiations. They were taken as war booty. They ended up far from their villages of origin, performing unpaid household labor and herding animals; some were sexually abused by their masters. We, and many other researchers, have only the stories of those who managed to escape or were freed, who represent the tip of the iceberg.

Many captured women and children were not bought or sold but simply kept by the soldiers or militia members who captured them. The fact that some were not sold in a market does not mean that the practice is not slavery. During Roman times slavery was often the fate of people taken as prisoners of war. The current practice of

---

[47] The Popular Defense Force (PDF) is a government militia which receives training from the army, although its training lasts only forty-five days and includes religious indoctrination: militia members are to become *mujahedeen* (holy warriors) engaged in *jihad* (holy war). Service in the PDF is required in addition to national army service for those who would enter university and for civil servants. Unlike the national army, women as well as men are expected to serve. The PDF will be discussed in an upcoming report.

capturing persons during the war and not selling them but keeping them as unpaid servants is not so very different from ancient practices.

Historically, according to one authority, the special characteristics of slavery:

> included the idea that slaves were property; that they were outsiders who were alien by origin or who had been denied their heritage through judicial or other sanctions; that coercion could be used at will; that their labour power was at the complete disposal of a master; that they did not have the right to their own sexuality and, by extension, to their own reproductive capacities; and that the slave status was inherited unless provision was made to ameliorate that status.[48]

Although the current practices in Sudan do not include all these special characteristics of slavery, they do include several: that slaves are outsiders, alien by origin (southern and Nuba African peoples), that coercion can be used on them at will, and that their labor power is at the complete disposal of a master.

Such is the cultural arrogance of some who take possession of these children that they may honestly feel that they are doing the children a favor by giving them a place in an Arab home, even as unpaid servants. For others, the convenience of unpaid docile child labor is too great to resist, especially since the authorities rarely condemn, investigate or punish the practice.

The Applicable Law
Slavery

Slavery is anathema in international law. The Universal Declaration of Human Rights provides in Article 4, " No one shall be held in slavery or servitude; slavery and the slave trade shall be prohibited in all their forms." This right is termed

---

[48] Paul E. Lovejoy, *Transformations in slavery* (Cambridge: Cambridge University Press, 1983), p. 1 (footnote omitted). Some authorities point out that the provision about slaves being "alien" in origin is probably not universally applicable, although it is applicable in many contexts, particularly in Africa.

"the cornerstone of all human rights,"[49] and slavery and servitude are so universally condemned that there is no doubt that customary international law prohibits them.[50]

In acceding to the 1926 Slavery Convention, as amended,[51] Sudan agreed to prevent and suppress the slave trade and to bring about the complete abolition of slavery in all its forms. It also agreed to take all necessary measures to prevent compulsory or forced labor from developing into conditions analogous to slavery.

Slavery was defined in that Convention in Article 1 (1) as "the status or condition of a person over whom *any* or all of the powers attaching to the right of ownership are exercised." (Emphasis supplied) One power attaching to the right of ownership is the power to completely dispose of the (unpaid) labor of the slave, which was exercised in the cases described below. One authority notes, "The term 'slavery' is technical and limited in scope, inasmuch as it implies ownership as chattel by another person and 'the destruction of the juridical personality.'"[52]

The slave trade was defined as including "all acts involved in the capture, acquisition or disposal of a person with intent to reduce him to slavery." Article 1 (2). The common denominator of slavery, slave trade, and servitude, as distinct from forced or compulsory labor, is that they are forbidden irrespective of the consent of the person concerned, or of his or her relatives.[53]

---

[49] Cited in Richard B. Lillich, "Chapter 4: Civil Rights," in ed. Theodor Meron, *Human Rights in International Law* (Oxford: Clarendon Press, 1988), p. 124.

[50] Ibid., p. 125. The prohibition against slavery and servitude now constitutes *jus cogens*, whereby it is binding even on those states which are not parties to the slavery conventions.

[51] 1926 Slavery Convention, amended in 1953. Text reprinted in Edward Lawson, *Encyclopedia of Human Rights* (Taylor & Francis, Inc., New York: 1991), pp. 1356-57, 1243-44.

[52] Yoram Dinstein, "Right to Life, Physical Integrity, and Liberty," in Louis Henkin, ed., *The International Bill of Rights* (Columbia University Press, New York: 1981), p. 126 (footnote omitted).

[53] Ibid.

In the 1956 Supplementary Convention on the Abolition of Slavery, the Slave Trade, and Institutions and Practices Similar to Slavery,[54] Article 5 states that in a country where the abandonment of slavery is not yet complete:

> the act of mutilating, branding or otherwise marking a slave or a person of servile status in order to indicate his status . . . shall be a criminal offence under the laws of the States Parties to this Convention and persons convicted thereof shall be liable to punishment.

In a case described below, a master branded a girl in case she was "lost."

Besides the specific conventions banning slavery and the slave trade that had their origins in the anti-slavery movement of the nineteenth century, regional and international conventions also ban slavery.[55] The African Charter provides in Article 5:

> Every individual shall have the right to the respect of the dignity inherent in a human being and to the recognition of his legal status. All forms of exploitation and degradation of man, particularly slavery, slave trade, torture, cruel, inhuman or degrading punishment and treatment shall be prohibited.

A nonderogable right in the International Covenant on Civil and Political Rights is the right to be free from slavery, in Article 8:

> 1. No one shall be held in slavery; slavery and the slave-trade in all their forms shall be prohibited.
> 2. No one shall be held in servitude.

---

[54] Sudan acceded to the Supplementary Convention on the Abolition of Slavery, the Slave Trade, and Institutions and Practices Similar to Slavery. Text reprinted in Lawson, *Encyclopedia of Human Rights*, pp. 1414-17.

[55] The Cairo Declaration on Human Rights in Islam, signed by the Organization of the Islamic Conference on August 5, 1990, was a proposal prepared by the 19th Islamic Conference of Ministers of Foreign Affairs held in Cairo in 1990. The proposal was presented to the conference of Kings and Presidents of the Islamic States, but they could not reach agreement on the declaration and as a result it was not ratified by any state. It states in Article 11 (a): "Human beings are born free, and no one has the right to enslave, humiliate, oppress or exploit them, and there can be no subjugation but to God the Most-High."

The 1956 Supplementary Convention on the Abolition of Slavery obliges the parties to "communicate to the Secretary-General of the United Nations copies of any laws, regulations and administrative measure enacted or put into effect to implement the provisions of this convention." The Economic and Social Council is to use this documentation as a basis for further recommendations on slavery.[56] These are not reporting requirements as such; Anti-Slavery International (formerly the Anti-Slavery Society) complained that there is no reporting requirement and labeled this a significant shortcoming of the 1956 Supplementary Convention on the Abolition of Slavery. This lack of proper reporting requirements may explain in part why Sudan has taken few steps to live up to its obligations under the Convention.

The Convention on the Rights of the Child, which Sudan ratified, requires that "in all actions taken regarding children, whether by public or private social welfare institutions, courts of law, administrative authorities or legislative bodies, the best interests of the child shall be a primary consideration." (Article 3 (1)) In two of the three individual cases described below, the police and prosecutors and criminal court judges did not seem to make the welfare of the child a primary consideration.

Forced Labor and Child Labor

The practices described below also qualify as forced or compulsory labor, defined in article 2 (1) of the 1930 Convention (No. 29) concerning Forced or Compulsory Labor,[57] to which Sudan has acceded, as

> all work or service which is exacted from any person under the menace of any penalty and for which the said person has not offered himself voluntarily.

The International Covenant on Civil and Political Rights also bans forced labor in Article 8 (3) (a): "No one shall be required to perform forced or compulsory labour."

The Convention on the Rights of the Child also obliges the government to protect children from economic exploitation, in Art. 32:

---

[56] Meron, ed., *Human Rights in International Law*, p. 375.

[57] Convention (ILO No. 29) concerning Forced or Compulsory Labour. Text reprinted in *International Labor Conventions and Recommendations, Vol. I* (Geneva: ILO, 1992), pp. 115-26. Sudan also acceded to Convention (ILO No. 105) concerning the Abolition of Forced Labour. Text reprinted in *International Labor Conventions and Recommendations, Vol. I* , pp. 618-19

> 1. States Parties recognize the right of the child to be protected from economic exploitation and from performing any work that is likely. . . to interfere with the child's education, or to be harmful to the child's health or physical, mental, spiritual, moral or social development.
> 2. States Parties shall take legislative, administrative, social and educational measures to ensure the implementation of this article. To this end, and having regard to the relevant provisions of other international instruments, States Parties shall in particular:
>   A. Provide for a minimum age or minimum ages for admissions to employment;
>   B. Provide for appropriate regulation of the hours and conditions of employment; and
>   C. Provide for appropriate penalties or other sanctions to ensure the effective enforcement of this article.

Other state duties also disregarded include the duty to take measures to protect the child from all forms of abuse, including trafficking in children,[58] and the duty to protect and care for children affected by armed conflict.[59] Sudan has not ratified the ILO Minimum Age Convention of 1973 (No. 138).

U.N. Proceedings Against Sudan on Slavery and Forced Labor, and the Government's Response

In an attempt to hold Sudan accountable for the slavery-like practices, certain practices "resembling slavery in their effects," occurring in the armed conflict in the south, were brought to the attention of the U.N. Working Group on Contemporary Forms of Slavery[60] by the Anti-Slavery Society in 1988. The practices described were

---

[58] Convention on the Rights of the Child, Arts. 19 and 35.

[59] Ibid, Art. 38 (4).

[60] In 1975 the United Nations created a Working Group on Contemporary Forms of Slavery to monitor the application of the slavery conventions. This group, which consists of five independent experts from the membership of the Sub-Commission on Prevention of Discrimination and Protection of Minorities, holds an annual meeting, with representatives of member states, other U.N. agencies, and accredited nongovernmental organizations in attendance. The Working Group on Contemporary Forms of Slavery was formed under the Sub-Committee on Prevention of Discrimination and Protection of Minorities, which is a sub-
(continued...)

the taking of Dinka slaves by tribal militias, sale and ransom of Dinka captives, and sale or pawning of children by destitute parents.[61] This information came in part from a study first published in Arabic by two Sudanese human rights activists and university professors.[62] The Sudan government denied that slavery or forced labor exists.

The U.N. Working Group did not consider this information at its 1988 session because "an understanding had been reached between the [Anti-Slavery] society and the government of Sudan for a fact-finding visit to be made to that country in order to obtain more precise information on the subject."[63] That fact-finding visit by the Anti-Slavery Society never took place. The military coup of June 30, 1989 intervened and the new government refused to cooperate with the mission. The matter is still pending. The next meeting of the U.N. Working Group should be in April 1996.

In 1993, when the U.N. Committee on the Rights of the Child raised questions about child slavery, the Sudan government stated that the situations described as slavery actually "involve tribal disputes and arguments over pasture and water resources in some areas where there is an overlap between tribes."[64] The government characterized the complained-of practices not as slavery but more like hostage-taking, where each tribe captured members of the other while waiting for the conflict to be settled through negotiations.

This type of hostage-taking may well occur, but these are not the facts of the cases we and others have researched. Our cases involve forced labor for no money under pain of physical punishment, after capture in war and separation from family and

---

(...continued)
committee of the U.N. Commission on Human Rights, under the U.N. Economic and Social Council.

[61] U.N. Economic and Social Council, Commission on Human Rights, Sub-Commission on Prevention of Discrimination and protection of Minorities, Working Group on Contemporary Forms of Slavery, Thirteenth session, "Review of Developments in the Field of Slavery and the Slave Trade in All Their Practices and Manifestations," E/CN.44/Sub.2/AC.2/1988/7/Add.1, document received from Anti-Slavery Society dated June 28, 1988 (Geneva: July 5, 1988). *See* Lawson, *Encyclopedia of Human Rights*, pp. 1413-14.

[62] Ushari Ahmad Mahmud and Suleyman Ali Baldo, "Human Rights Abuses in the Sudan 1987, Al Diein Massacre: Slavery in the Sudan" (English synopsis: 1987).

[63] Lawson, *Encyclopedia of Human Rights*, p. 1414.

[64] Sudan Submission of June 1993 to the CRC, p.11.

place of origin. In addition, in the cases described there was no negotiation in progress of an overarching tribal dispute that would involve release of the captured children and women.

The government of Sudan said in its June 1993 submission to the U.N. Committee on the Rights of the Child that, regarding slavery, "the government has drawn up a detailed reply for submission to the International Labour Office and the Commission on Human Rights."[65] The committee nevertheless stated in its report to the General Assembly, "Reports on the forced labor and slavery of children give cause for the Committee's deepest concern."[66]

The ILO, which works on the basis of the report of its committee of experts, has continued to consider the question of slavery or forced labor in the Sudan, most recently at its June 1993 conference. Its committee of experts took up the question again in 1994, requesting that the government of Sudan "provide full information on measures taken or envisaged to ensure the practical application of Article 25 of the Convention [ILO Forced Labor Convention, No. 29], and on measures taken to protect the Dinka and Nuba populations against practices contrary to the Convention."[67] The government was asked to report in detail for the period ending June 30, 1994.

The U.N. Human Rights Commission's Special Rapporteur on Human Rights in Sudan has documented numerous reports of abduction and forced removal of people for purposes of slavery.[68] In addition, there are reports by human rights groups and the press of slavery since his last report.[69]

The Sudan government produced a report to the ILO in 1994 in Arabic; this appears to be the report on allegations of slavery and forced labor to which the government referred in its June 1993 submission to the U.N. Committee on the Rights of the Child. It does not appear to have been sent to the U.N. Commission on Human

---

[65] Ibid.

[66] United Nations, Report of the Committee on the Rights of the Child, General Assembly, 49th Session, Suppl. No. 41, A/49/41 (New York: United Nations, 1994), p. 44.

[67] International Labor Organization, Report of the Committee of Experts: Observations Concerning Ratified Conventions: Sudan, 81st ILC, 1994, C.29, Report III (4A), p. 132.

[68] Special Rapporteur Biró, Report of February 1994, pp. 16-18, 30-32; *see* Special Rapporteur Biró, Report of January 1995, pp. 3-4.

[69] Christian Solidarity International, "Visit to Sudan, May 31-June 5, 1995," London, June 1995; Tim Sandler, "Africa's invisible slaves," *The Boston Phoenix*, June 30-July 6, 1995, pp. 16-20; Shyam Bhatia, "Sudan revives the slave trade," *The Observer* (London), April 9, 1995.

Rights.[70] Its translation from the Arabic was received by the ILO only in December 1994, too late to be considered at the February 1995 meeting of its committee of experts. This committee of experts may reconsider the question in its November-December 1995 meeting. Its next report to the ILO Conference is for the June 1996 meeting.[71]

Sudan points to its own legislation criminalizing forced labor.[72] The 1991 Criminal Code punishes forced labor, but the penalty is only one year's imprisonment and a possible fine.[73] There does not appear to be section in the Criminal Code specifically mentioning slavery.

As to the implementation of that article on forced labor, the ILO committee of experts took note of the government's reply: "As concerned ordinary courts the Attorney General had advised that no case of this nature existed as shown from their records."[74] The Workers' members of the International Labor Conference commented that such a penal code, "for which no information was available on its application, was merely a formal instrument."[75]

The Sudan government further told the ILO that a committee responsible for investigating the allegations referred to had been formed, and "had made several visits

---

[70] Under ILO Rules, this government report is not available to the public but its contents are summarized in the committee of experts and conference proceedings. No summary is yet available to the public.

[71] Telephone interview, ILO, Geneva, August 2, 1995.

[72] Other relevant Criminal Code articles concern kidnaping (art. 162) and unlawful confinement (art. 164): "162. Whoever kidnaps any person by compelling him or by any means of deceit induces him to leave a certain place, with intent to commit an offence on his person or his liberty, shall be punished with imprisonment for a term not exceeding ten years or with fine or with both. . . 164. Whoever confines any person by intentionally obstructing him so as to prevent his movement, or unlawfully changes his direction, shall be punished with imprisonment for a term not exceeding three months or with fine or with both."

[73] The Criminal Code of 1991: "Forced Labor/163. Whoever commits forced labour on any person by unlawfully compelling him to work against his will, shall be punished with imprisonment for a term not exceeding one year or with fine or with both."

[74] International Labor Conference, Report of the Committee of Experts: Sudan, 81st ILC, 1994, C.29, Report III (4A), p. 130.

[75] International Labor Conference, Report of the Conference Committee on the Application of Conventions and Recommendations: Sudan, 80th ILC, 1993, pp. 25/28.

to the regions involved, without having noticed any evidence of the truth of the allegations."[76] The U.N. Committee on the Rights of the Child, emphasizing "the need to pay urgent and due regard to the reports of forced labour and slavery of children," stated, "The Committee believes that international cooperation, particularly technical assistance and advice, could be used to that end."[77] The government has yet to seek such assistance and advice.

Group and Individual Cases

The group case we describe below has had a fortunate ending for the more than 500 captured women and children: a southern police officer was able to detach them from their military captors when they passed through his jurisdiction. Cases recorded by others this year illustrate, however, that those saved by official intervention continue to be in the minority.

Two 1995 reports[78] list recent testimonies, including allegations that there was:

- a group of 282 Dinka taken as slaves following a murahiliin/army/PDF raid on Nyamlell, Bahr El Ghazal, on March 25, 1995. Forty-eight of those enslaved were children. Some of them were sold off at the markets in Marein and Daiein, and others in Manyeil eight miles west of Nyamlell, where one Arab trader regularly turns up with local children for sale. Some of the children were bought back by their families there and perhaps half those enslaved managed to escape and return home;

- a slave market conducted in May 1994 at Manyeil which a girl captured in a raid on Marial Bai in Bahr El Ghazal in the late 1980s and 150 other children were sold. This girl was captured at age seven and taken to Darfur to live in her master's home, where she was beaten and had to work seven days a week. A Dinka paid one AKM rifle and a cow to buy her and set her free;

---

[76] Ibid.

[77] United Nations, Report of the Committee on the Rights of the Child, General Assembly 49th Session, Suppl. No. 41 (A/49/41), p. 44.

[78] Christian Solidarity International, "Visit to Sudan, May 31-June 5, 1995;" Tim Sandler, "Africa's invisible slaves," pp. 16-20. *See* African Rights, *Facing Genocide: The Nuba of Sudan*, pp. 211-12.

- a March 1995 raid on the Nuba village of Dere in which more than 300 women and children were abducted, and many taken to a slave market in El Lagowa, also in the Nuba Mountains; and

- an adult victim captured near Abiyei and kept in slavery from May 1994 until his escape in March 1995.

These new accounts, taken together with existing reports of slavery, demand further investigation by the Sudan government, the U.N. Committee on the Rights of the Child, UNICEF, the ILO, the Working Group on Contemporary Forms of Slavery, and the U.N. Commission Human Rights' Special Rapporteur on Sudan. Cases of slavery are notoriously difficult to research, since one must find freed slaves. In some cases, they gained their freedom by escaping, not by court order, and they remain fearful that their old masters will try to recapture them. Yet these cases, and the cases we found, require that the entire subject be fully investigated and the results be made public within Sudan.

The individual cases described below illustrate the typical circumstances—military raids—under which southern and Nuba children fall into the power of unrelated northerners who force the children to work for free in households hundreds or thousands of kilometers from their families or places of origin.[79] They also illustrate the harsh conditions of work and life imposed on the children, and how difficult it is for families to locate their children and pry them away from their exploiters.

In some cases, the children are not reunited with their families, but are rescued by southerners and others working anonymously to free enslaved southern children. Although we have received many detailed reports of individual cases of slavery, we include only ones we interviewed. The stories are remarkably consistent.

Children And Women Captured by Soldiers and PDF Then Freed by Southern Police in Bahr El Ghazal

We learned of the capture of more than 500 women and children by soldiers and Popular Defense Forces militia in Bahr El Ghazal in early 1995 that was thwarted by southern police in Aweil, demonstrating what the authorities can do to stop this practice if they have the will. The captures were made while the soldiers and the PDF were in the process of guarding a train moving slowly to Wau; as documented often

---

[79] Such raids by Baggara militias, armed by the local Umma Party powers, on the Dinkas, were part of a counterinsurgency strategy to strike at the SPLA by impoverishing their supposed Dinka kin and supporters. This has been the subject of extensive human rights reporting and scholarly works. *See* David Keen, *The Benefits of Famine: A Political Economy of Famine and Relief in Southwestern Sudan, 1983-1989* (Princeton, New Jersey: Princeton University Press, 1994).

elsewhere, they were conducting a scorched-earth campaign to clear civilians from the strategically important railway line. This campaign consisted not only in abduction of women and children, but also summary executions, use of civilians as hostages, rape, destruction of villages, and looting of cattle.[80] According to a well-informed source:

> A military- and militia-escorted train from Khartoum made its way in early 1995 to Wau; when it arrived in Wau in early May it had with it 3,000 cattle the soldiers and PDF had looted from the Dinka villages along the way.
>
> Unlike the two similar trains that arrived before it, however, this convoy did not bring any captured women or children.[81] The soldiers and militia had captured more than 500 women and children in the villages along the tracks, as usual, but they had been freed by a southern police colonel in Aweil.
>
> The convoy guards and the train had been attacked by the SPLA before reaching the Aweil area. The soldiers and militia fled with their loot into Aweil, seeking protection from the Aweil army base, instead of garrisoning themselves outside Aweil with their booty, as was their custom. Once inside Aweil, a police colonel by the name of John Garang (no relation to the head of the SPLA) stopped them and made them leave the women and children in Aweil. He permitted the soldiers and militia to take the cattle with them.[82]

What follows are summaries of the testimonies of some of the individual victims of other raids, and of the people who helped them.

---

[80] Amnesty International, *The Tears of Orphans*, p. 71.

[81] *See* Ibid., pp. 71-78.

[82] The cattle were sold in Wau at the train station by the soldiers and militia, after they reached Wau in early May. One cow was sold for one watch or one bicycle or tape recorder. The sons of the owners of the cattle followed the train and identified their stolen cattle to the police in Wau, but nothing was done for them and they did not get the cattle back. Interview, Khartoum, May 26, 1995.

Alang's Story

Alang Agak is free now after six years of unpaid labor, beatings, branding, a new Arab name in place of her Dinka name and forced conversion at the hands of her masters. She has, however, lost her father (who was killed in the raid during which she was captured in 1986 at age six), and her mother, Nyan Ajak Deng (who committed suicide on April 15, 1994, because the court case of her daughter had been delayed for so long). Her brother Ajang lost his job because he spent so much time tracing her and then in court, trying to have her returned to the family.

Criminal proceedings against her masters did not succeed because the masters brought in Dinka witnesses to declare that Alang was their child whom they "gave" to the masters. A civil proceeding (with positive blood grouping tests for her and her original family) resulted in a judgment in favor of her brother when the master's family failed to appear and contest the proceedings.[83]

> In 1986 the Arab militia attacked Alang's family's Dinka village, Low, outside of Abiyei in Southern Kordofan. Her mother tried to protect six-year-old Alang from being taken by the militia, but the mother was beaten on the head and fell down unconscious; the militias left her for dead and took the girl. Alang's father was killed in this raid.
>
> Her brother Ajang was working in Port Sudan when word reached him of Alang's kidnaping. He returned to the area where he learned that his father had died, and his mother's whereabouts were unknown. He did not dare to go directly to the Abiyei area since he had been warned that the army and Arab militias would kill him if they found him there. After a search, however, he found his other sister, Achol, and his mother.
>
> He took them to stay with relatives and continued to search for Alang in western Sudan. He moved among the Baggara cattle camps, which were open. He would go in, looking without asking, as if looking for a lost cow. When he did not find her there, he decided to go to Shendi because he heard that many Dinka from around Abiyei had been taken north to Shendi.

---

[83] Interviews, Khartoum, May 19, 1995.

In 1992, six years after she had been kidnaped, he traced Alang to an Arab family by the name of Salah (not their real name) west of Shendi in a place called Jebel Ab.

A Nuba living in Jebel Ab told Ajang that many Dinka children lived in that village, in the area of Metemma. Ajang and the Nuba man searched the goat-grazing areas where southern children were looking after the goats. Ajang recognized Alang because she "looks a lot like her sister."

He went over to her and talked to her. She said she did not know him. "If you want me, go to Salah," she said, giving him the name and address of her master.

Alang does not remember the kidnaping since she was young. She remembers being brought to Abu Lager, Kordofan, and living with the Salah family there. Her work was to clean the compound and rooms, fetch water, and wash dishes for the family.

Salah, his wife and adult son lived in that house; Alang slept outside. Whenever there was rain, they gave her a sack to protect herself. She had no bed. She ate the same food, but separately from the family. She did not go to school. When she refused to wash the dishes, she would be beaten with a whip used on animals.

She was never paid for her work.

The family left Abu Lager for Shendi "several years ago." Bad as it was, Abu Lager was better than Shendi for Alang. In Abu Lager she was still small and therefore not given too much work. In Jebel Ab she had more work, including the new task of looking after the goats.

In Jebel Ab, Alang slept in the kitchen on an old bed made of rope which was loose and touching the floor. She did not attend school. An aunt of the family tried to put Alang in school, but five days later Salah and his wife made her quit school. They said that if she learned, she would escape.

She also ate the same food as the family but separately; they ate *kasira*[84] with broth. She had kasira with water. She used to look after goats without having breakfast and sometimes she would not come back until 7 p.m., so she went the whole day without food.

They insulted her. They said she was a slave, had no father or mother, and called her a thief. The daughter who was Alang's age was not friendly to her; the only one who was kind to her sometimes was an older daughter.

They used to beat her with a chain used for bicycles. The beatings were administered by Salah's son, Abdullah (not his real name), who lived with them. She still has a scar on her back from one bad beating.

She was branded on the leg. The wife of Salah took a small iron pot with a fire inside, used to ward off flies, and turned it over on Alang's leg, to mark her "in case she got lost." She left two large scars on Alang's thigh near the knee.

They asked her to become a Muslim. She said she did not know how to do that. They asked her to pray but she did not know why she was praying. They gave her another name, Toma Kaputera (teapot). She did not know her real name while she was living with this family. When she lived with this family, she forgot how to speak Dinka.

After he located her, Alang's brother Ajang lodged a complaint with the Shendi police and the matter was investigated. While the case was pending from 1992-94, his mother, who never recovered completely from the beating by the murahiliin, took her own life.

Ajang opened a police case against Salah and Abdullah. The police registered his information and Ajang was asked to bring a car to take two police to Jebel Ab. The police arrested Abdullah and brought him and Alang, who was by then twelve years old, to Shendi.

---

[84] Kasira is a pancake-like thin bread made from sorghum flour, typical of Sudan.

They were all detained in the police station. The next morning the police referred the information to the attorney general's office. The prosecutor ordered the girl to return to Jebel Ab and said that the process would take place while she was living at the Salah family home.

The brother rejected this, saying that Alang should stay with the prosecutor if he wanted, or else be left on bond with a Dinka elder. After some argument, the prosecutor permitted the girl to stay with the Dinka elder, with an undertaking.

Abdullah denied the charges against him. He traveled to Abu Lager to find Salah at his job and bring him back to testify in Shendi.

Salah claimed that he "bought the girl" from a Dinka family, Deng Akon and Akuol Akon (not their real names), "in front of the court at Abu Lager." There were witnesses to the purchase, he said, and produced a letter supposedly from the court in Abu Lager. He handed the letter to the prosecutor, who tore it up on the spot and told him not to talk of this again. (The price supposedly paid was not discovered by the brother.)

Then Salah's family, which was allegedly related to the prosecutor and received advice from him, came up with the story that Alang was the daughter of Deng, who "gave" her to Salah.

The prosecutor then ordered that the girl be handed over to Deng, although the matter was still under investigation and had not been brought to a court. The brother rejected this and said he would fight and die first. "If someone wants her, let them come to where we are." He refused to deliver her to the Deng family.

The district attorney ordered the case transferred to Abu Lager for trial. The brother appealed to the senior prosecutor who reversed this decision and ordered a trial at Shendi. The junior prosecutor remained hostile.

The first sitting of the trial was on June 7, 1993, in Shendi. The defense claimed the family of Salah had hired a Dinka woman, Akuol Akon, and her husband Deng Akon, to work for them. It was claimed that this girl was their daughter. The accused claimed that the girl had been "given" to them by this Dinka family. Salah brought the Dinka family to Shendi to give this false testimony in the case.

In December 1994, the court ruled that there was no evidence to show that the girl had been kidnaped; there were no eyewitnesses, so the accused were acquitted.

The brother, Ajang, was working in Port Sudan with a maintenance company. He finished eighth grade but did not go further because of these family problems. He is the sole support of his mother and sisters. The whole family moved to Shendi for the proceedings since it was too expensive to come and go from Port Sudan. Ultimately he lost his job because of his absences related to freeing his sister.

After the court decided there was no proof of kidnaping, the family went to the civil court to contest the matter. They asked for help from a church, which referred them to an attorney.

The civil case filed in Khartoum was decided on technical grounds: Deng Akon was summoned to the Khartoum court but did not appear so he lost by default. In this civil proceeding a blood grouping test was performed in a hospital and it was found that Alang was in the same blood group as her mother and sister. Alang was awarded to her brother Ajang.

"Mabior's" Story

An eight-year-old Dinka was captured by a soldier during a military raid on his village near Bor in 1988. He and another boy were taken by that soldier to his home in Wad Medani, where they were given new Arab names, were forced to work for no pay and were sexually abused by their soldier-master. When they were able to complain to a Dinka they saw in the market, a criminal complaint was made on their behalf. Soldier friends of their master then removed the two boys from official custody to their army base, however, where the boys were threatened.

The police erred in permitting the soldiers to remove the boys from police custody. As a result of the threats the boys did not speak up at the hearing before the prosecutor the following day. When an appeal was not possible, concerned persons took matters into their own hands and snatched the boys away, according to the victim and a reliable source whose testimonies are summarized below. [85]

> Mabior (not his real name), a Bor Dinka, lived with his family in Marang, to the west of Bor. After a Nuer or SPLA factional raid devastated Marang in 1991 or 1992, government troops arrived in Bor and Marang in 1992, by which time there was no food in the village. Mabior was eight years old.
>
> The army soldiers surrounded the Marang school early one morning and assembled the children in one place. They put the children into army lorries and trucked them to Bor, although some children managed to escape.
>
> An army officer named Abdelrahman (not his real name) brought Mabior and another boy, Agar (not his real name), to Bor. The captured children were placed in a Koranic school. When Abdelrahman was transferred to Wad Medani, he took Mabior and Agar with him, and gave them Arab names when they reached Wad Medani: Mabior was renamed Omer Abdelrahman and Agar became Abdullah Abdelrahman.
>
> Abdelrahman, an unmarried man, placed the two boys in the home of his mother in Wad Medani, where his adult brothers and sister also lived. There were no other children in the house.
>
> Mabior stayed "a long time" in that house. There were times when he was treated well, also times when he was treated badly. The two captured Dinka boys slept in one bed. They were given leftovers to eat.
>
> The two Dinka boys did all the housework. They received no money for their work. Among their chores were mopping the floor, washing dishes and clothes, dusting, and going to market. Abdelrahman beat them if they did not do things like empty the runoff water from the bath.

---

[85] Interviews, Khartoum, May 19, 1995.

Abdelrahman sexually abused his two captives. When he came home from work, he would take off his clothes and begin the abuse. They did not know where to go to complain since they did not know Wad Medani at all. Abdelrahman would also insult them, saying that their people were "bad, primitive" and other insults that Mabior was too ashamed to repeat.

When the two boys went to the market one day, they saw a young Dinka man. They explained their living conditions to him and gave him their real names. He sent information to Khartoum that there was a boy by his name in Wad Medani. In Khartoum one man, Joseph (not his real name), who assisted families trying to recover their kidnaped children, received this information as well as the information that many children had been brought from Bor to Wad Medani. He went to Wad Medani and located the two boys in the market, in or around 1994, when Mabior was about ten.

Joseph returned to Khartoum and sought legal advice about the sexual abuse to which Abdelrahman was subjecting the boys. The court was petitioned and an investigation initiated by the police in Wad Medani, who came to Abdelrahman's house and took the boys to the police station. On that day, Abdelrahman was in Kosti. That night a relative of Abdelrahman came to the police station with soldier friends of Abdelrahman who told the police that these were "our" boys, whom they had brought from Bor, and now they wanted to take them. The police released the boys to the soldiers.

The boys were taken to the army base, where they spent the night. The soldiers and Abdelrahman's relatives there intimidated the boys. They said that when the boys were in front of the court, the judge would be a northerner, "like us," and would decide "in our favor," that the boys should remain with Abdelrahman. The relatives threatened the boys that if they "made a mistake and said they wanted to go with Joseph," they would be released to Abdelrahman all the same and Abdelrahman would return and kill them. The best course was to "deny Joseph."

The prosecutor of Wad Medani asked the army to produce the boys at his office. He (not a judge) then asked the boys if they knew Joseph and if they wanted to go with him.

The boys, mindful of the threats, said that they did not know Joseph and they did not want to go with him. The prosecutor then ordered the children back to Abdelrahman's custody and said that Joseph should open a civil (not a criminal) case.

The case was appealed to the Attorney General in Khartoum, who unsuccessfully asked for the case file to be sent to him from Wad Medani. Joseph went to Wad Medani, where he was threatened and was told that the papers were lost.

Concerned persons then took the law into their own hands. They captured the two boys in Wad Medani and brought them to Khartoum, where they have been living in freedom ever since.

Mabior was the youngest of four brothers; he is now still separated from them and his mother as well (his father was already dead by the time of the 1992 raid in which Mabior was captured). One brother also was trucked to Bor but they were separated when Abdelrahman took Mabior away. His whereabouts are unknown. Another two brothers are "somewhere in the south."

"Akom's" Story

A Dinka boy, Akom (not his real name), was captured in 1988, when he was five. He was captured by Arab Baggara militia during a raid on his village, Majung Akom, near Aweil in northern Bahr El Ghazal. After five years of cruel treatment by the family of the militiaman who captured him, for whom he performed unpaid labor in southern Kordofan, he escaped to the nearby city of El Muglad. There a man from Shendi in northern Sudan took him into his home, first in El Muglad and then Shendi, also to work for free. When he was badly beaten repeatedly by his master's son in Shendi, he escaped from that house.

When the master's son discovered his whereabouts and took him to the police to ask them to force the boy to return to his master, a southern policeman intervened and arranged for Akom to stay with a local Dinka community leader instead.[86]

At the time of the Arab Baggara militia raid on his village in 1988, Akom was playing in an open area of the village. He saw people in

---

[86] Interviews, Khartoum, May 19, 1995.

uniform approaching but he did not run because he thought they were SPLA rebel soldiers, who were often around but did not raid the villages.

An Arab Baggara militiaman (*murahiliin*) by the name of Malek (not his real name) rode up on a horse and grabbed him. Akom was the only member of his family who was captured but the murahiliin took other Dinka boys as well as many head of cattle. He has not seen his mother since; his father died before Akom's capture. Akom does not remember if he had brothers or sisters.

He was taken by his captor to Sitib, a small village near El Muglad town in Southern Kordofan. There he lived with Malek, his captor, and Malek's family (including three children smaller than Akom) in a tent settlement. He did not know Arabic when he was captured and but he learned it from this family during the more than five years they kept him in Sitib. He was given a *jellabia* to wear.[87]

Akom's job was to look after the animals of the master. He was never paid for his work. While he received the same food as the family, he ate alone most of the time. He does not know why they fed him separately. He did not attend school.

The treatment he received from the family was "not good." The worst part of his treatment was the lashing, administered as punishment when he would lose one of the goats or sheep he was tending. He was beaten with a branch of a tree.[88]

Using Dinka children to herd animals was common in this area. While he was looking after the animals, he would encounter other Dinka boys doing the same job for other masters. There were "many" of them and they spoke in Dinka to each other. This was not traditionally a Dinka area.

---

[87] The *jellabia* is a long white robe worn by men. In southern Sudan it is considered to be typical of the northerners. The men who wear this robe are referred to as *jellaba* all over Sudan, meaning migrants (often traders) from northern Sudan.

[88] The children of the family were not beaten at all. Nor did they look after the goats and sheep, since they were too small.

The treatment he received in Malek's home was so bad that he finally fled when he was big enough, that is, ten years old. He escaped to El Muglad, which he had heard people talk about as "a big town." He walked two days to El Muglad, eating only wild fruit along the way.

In El Muglad he went to the market where on the first day he encountered a man by the name of Omar (not his real name) who called to him and asked about his parents. Akom replied that they were "in the Dinka area." Omar asked him if he was working with anyone, and Akom said no. Omar asked if Akom wanted to work in his house, and the boy agreed. Omar never paid him for his work.

Akom stayed for three months in El Muglad, working in Omar's house, where the two lived alone. Omar did not beat him. Omar gave Akom a bed, and he slept inside the house. He cleaned the house, washed the dishes, and shopped for food in the market.

Omar, who was in El Muglad because he worked at the White Nile Oil Company there, then took Akom to Shendi, Omar's place of origin, where he had three grown children. Shendi is about 1,230 kilometers from El Muglad.

Akom stayed in Omar's home in Shendi for five months. He had a bed, received the same food as the rest of the family, and ate with them. But these were bad times nevertheless, because Abdullah (not his real name), Omar's thirty-year-old son, a big man, beat Akom and slapped his face frequently. Akom would be beaten when he refused to wash clothes or clean the floor.

Abdullah used to call Akom "slave," and also *jangawi*, a pejorative term for Dinka.

Akom was frequently sent to the market and in general had more work in Shendi than in El Muglad. Four adults and a boy his age, Rahman (not his real name), lived in the house Akom was expected to clean. The boy Rahman, Omar's son, was good to Akom. They became friends. But Rahman was not beaten and he went to school; Akom did not go to school.

Akom escaped once from the house, but not knowing anyone else in Shendi, he went to the bakery where he was sent to shop. He stayed at the bakery with the Nuba who ran it for two days. When Abdullah went to the bakery he spotted Akom, and called on him to return to the house. Akom resisted, but Abdullah caught him and pulled him down the street. Akom cried and Abdullah dragged him to the police station.

At the police station, Abdullah asked the police to order Akom to return to the house with him. He said that Akom was working for his family and that Omar had brought the boy from southern Sudan. Omar's family could not allow Akom to move around Shendi freely because they were responsible for Akom, Abdullah said.

The police asked Akom if he was ready to return to Abdullah's house. Akom said no, he was ill-treated there, and they were not even his relatives. The police told Abdullah that the boy should stay with them at the police station. <u>Fortunately for Akom, as for so many other southerners living in the north, one of the police was a Dinka named Wilson.</u>

Wilson contacted Majur, a Dinka community leader in Shendi, and handed Akom over to Majur to look after. Akom stayed in Majur's home for about a week.

In the meantime, another Dinka in Khartoum who traced kidnaped southern children was notified. As a result, Akom, although not yet reunited with his family, is now enrolled in school and lives with other boys under adult supervision, with a bed to sleep on and no more unpaid household labor.

4
RECRUITMENT FOR THE NATIONAL MILITARY SERVICE OF UNDERAGE BOYS AND VIOLATION OF THEIR FREEDOM OF RELIGION

Underage children have been drafted as soldiers and required to fight, in violation of the Convention on the Rights of the Child[89] and Sudanese law, which sets eighteen as the minimum age. In one case, we found that a ten-year-old Dinka boy had been drafted into a Mundari tribal militia by government forces in 1991 and kept in service until he escaped in 1995.

Government officials persist in characterizing the current civil war as an Islamic "holy war" against the south, although many of the young men required by law to serve in the army and fight in this war are not Muslims and are southerners. Freedom of religion is a nonderogable right under the International Covenant on Civil and Political Rights, Article 18; under the Convention on the Rights of the Child, Article 14; and under the African Charter, Article 8. The way in which religious studies are introduced in the context of training military recruits subjects the conscripts to coercion which would impair their freedom to have a religion of their own choice. Nor are the non-Muslim recruits given an equal opportunity to manifest their religion on the same basis as are the Muslim recruits, which violates Article 2 of the same Covenant.[90]

---

[89] Convention on the Rights of the Child, Art. 38 (2): "States Parties shall take all feasible measures to ensure that persons who have not attained the age of 15 years do not take a direct part in hostilities." Fifteen years is the minimum age for recruitment under international humanitarian law as reflected in Protocols I and II of 1977 to the Four Geneva Conventions of 1949.

The Convention on the Rights of the Child, Art. 38 (3), further stipulates that when recruiting among those who have attained the age of fifteen but not yet attained the age of eighteen years, State Parties are under an obligation to give priority to those who are oldest in its recruitment efforts.

Human Rights Watch's position is that no one under the age of eighteen should take part in armed conflict. Human Rights Watch supports the efforts of the United Nations Working Group on a Draft Optional Protocol to the Convention on the Rights of the Child on the Involvement of Children in Armed Conflict that would raise the age at which people can take part in armed conflict from fifteen to eighteen.

[90] International Covenant on Civil and Political Rights, Article 2 (1): "Each State Party to the present Covenant undertakes to respect and to ensure to all individuals within its territory . . .
(continued...)

President Lt.-Gen. Omar al-Bashir, on January 1, 1995, in Port Sudan, called upon the citizens to join the popular defense training camps, which this year would witness the training of "more than one million recruits to defend the country against the machinations of the enemies lying in wait to detract from its unity and sovereignty."[91] But the government was not relying only upon the PDF. In early 1995 there also was widespread military conscription of young men which lead to serious abuses, including the drafting of underage boys.

A call went out from the National Service for young men between the ages of eighteen and thirty-three to register for compulsory army service. This call was largely ignored; of the 10,000 notices mailed out, only eighty-nine young men came forward, according to Minister of Defense Jasam Abdel-Rahman Ali's statement to the Transitional National Assembly (TNA) on May 31, 1995, after it demanded an explanation for the unpopular recruitment going on at checkpoints in Khartoum.[92] The minister of defense said that the government had tried for two years to conscript all males between those two ages, a total of about 2.5 million people. Up to early June 1995 only 26,079 out of the 2.5 million had turned up for training and of those only 12,541 had completed the course.[93]

Part of the reason for the draft evasion is no doubt historical: the army, in its British origins during colonial times, was a volunteer professional army. National conscription was never seriously undertaken until the current government came into office; conscription legislation passed in 1972 during Nimeiri's regime was never enforced. In 1992 the president issued a law requiring at least one year's military training for those in the eighteen to thirty-three age group.[94]

(...continued)
the rights recognized in the present Covenant, without distinction of any kind, such as . . . religion . . . or other status."

[91] "Bashir says one million popular defense recruits to be trained this year," Republic of Sudan Radio, Omdurman, in Arabic, 1 Jan. 1995, quoted in ME/2191 MED/19 (SWB, January 3, 1995).

[92] Reuter News Service, "Sudanese Rounding Up Draft-Dodgers in Khartoum," Khartoum, June 5, 1995. The Transitional National Assembly performs some legislative functions but is appointed by the president, not elected.

[93] Ibid.

[94] Ibid.

The minister of defense also admitted that due to pressure from the war in southern Sudan, since 1992 the government has started forcing government and private sector workers in that age bracket to join the army. This failed to bring in enough conscripts, and lead in March 1995 to government efforts to impress young men that the government admitted were very unpopular. [95] These efforts included army officials, assisted by members of the PDF, setting up checkpoints throughout the city, with tents serving as mobile offices where they could examine the identity papers of all draft-age men.

Reportedly boys as young as twelve were collected, not only from public buses and other vehicles but also at football stadiums and other recreation centers. During March mothers swarmed to the recruiting tents in search of their sons.

The street children's camps became a convenient reservoir from which to draw army conscripts; many maintain that they were created in part to serve that purpose. If so, then the parallels with the SPLA underage recruitment practice are striking. One boy then fourteen years of age describes below how such recruitment was carried out from a street children's camp in late 1994. Although the boys could decline to volunteer for the army, many whom the custodians of the street children's camp solicited for military service were well below the legal age of eighteen.

Recruitment efforts were not limited to the north, however. We received one report that the government raided and burned villages east of Kadugli and around Buram in the Nuba Mountains and, among other things, forcibly collected 600 Nuba boys between the ages of nine and fourteen. They reportedly took them to Kadugli and a few days later to Um Ruaba for Islamic religious instruction at the Khalwa of Sheikh Bakri Wagiealla Mohammed Kheir.[96]

The army also forcibly drafted underage southerners in garrison towns to fight against their fellow southerners in the SPLA. In Juba in January 1995, a seventeen-year-old school boy was captured with thirteen others from where they were swimming in the Nile, and flown north for a brutal regime of military training and forced Islamic studies. This was despite the fact that he should have been exempted from the draft under Sudanese law since he was a full-time student and under the age of eighteen. No notice whatsoever was given to the boys' families.

---

[95] KNA news agency, Nairobi, June 2, 1995, "Sudan: Defense Minister Reportedly Admits Some 'Errors' During Roundups for Military Service," carried by BBC Monitoring Service: Middle East, June 5, 1995.

[96] The source of this information wishes to remain anonymous. He produced a list of forty-four names of boys who were sent to the Khalwa at Um Ruaba. *See* African Rights, *Facing Genocide*, pp. 257-58 (over one hundred children removed from Um Dorein in March 1995).

While the army does not admit recruiting children under eighteen years of age, it is no secret that there are army schools in the larger garrisons where children of soldiers are given regular schooling and learn a trade. They wear the uniform and are held under quasi-military discipline and usually volunteer for military service when they reach the legal age.

The government also denied allegations that it was rushing young conscripts into war zones shortly after induction, and that many untrained youth were being killed in battle due to inexperience. There are reports that some young soldiers who have fought in the south are being treated for mental and physical injuries in Omdurman Military Hospital.

According to the minister of defense, under Sudanese military law conscripts will be sent to the battlefield only if they opt to do so willingly. He said that they had sent only 1,850 recruits to the "operations zones," all at their own request; not more than fifty-four of them had been killed in action.[97]

The provision that draftees can only go into combat if they do so at their own request is highly unusual in a country at war: the law is not honored, however. A group of 750 conscripts was posted directly to Juba, the largest garrison town in the south, upon graduating from a two-month military training course in April 1995, according to a reliable source. Several protested on the grounds that the authorities had promised them in February 1995, at the start of their training, that they would be posted to combat zones only if they wanted to go there. Those complaining were threatened with jail if they persisted in their protests. The 750 conscripts chosen for the war zone were all those from the graduating class who did not have university degrees.

"James'" Story

In 1991 Government army forces captured James (not his real name), a Dinka from the Yirol district on the West Bank of the Nile, and inducted him into a tribal militia; at the time he was about nine or ten years old. He was kept in military service for almost four years, until he escaped in 1995, when he was thirteen or fourteen.[98] While he was in training near Khartoum, Christians were proselytized by army trainers and not permitted to practice their religion. We summarize his testimony below:[99]

---

[97] KNA news agency,"Sudan: Defense Minister Reportedly Admits Some 'Errors' During Roundups for Military Service."

[98] Interview, Khartoum, May 19, 1995.

[99] Times are approximate.

The army captured James, a ten-year-old Dinka boy, during a spring 1991 skirmish between the army and the SPLA, followed by a government raid on the cattle camp near his village. The army soldiers took cattle and forty boys, big and small, who happened to be in the cattle camp when they raided it.

The officer who captured him was probably a member of the government-sponsored and -armed Mundari militia, which wore the same uniform as army soldiers. The Mundari militia had its own camp and ate army provisions. He knew only the name of the militia he was forced to join, Arenga. (The Mundari are an African people.)

He understood that "the larger boys were returned to the village because they were not useful." The soldiers brought twenty-five of the younger boys, including James, to a government military camp in Terekeka, north of Juba. The boys were kept for ten months in that camp and there taught the use of arms, military tactics, and other things. They did chores such as cut firewood, build *tukls* (huts) with mud, and fetch water from the Nile. Some of the twenty-five boys were younger and some older than he; at the time he was nine or ten.

During training four boys tried to escape. The army pursued them and presumably killed the four; although James did not see the bodies, the four had run away with four guns and the soldiers came back with four guns. The boys' names were Adut Twic, Matean, Ariop, and Ngong.

The army officers tried to give the boys religious instruction in Islam, but, said James, the boys were all Christian so they "resisted when the army tried to make us Muslims." The army did not push this; "they were not that serious about it in the south." It was a different story in the northern military camp.

In the Terekeka camp, the government soldiers physically disciplined the boys by beating or tying them. Sometimes the boys had to do extra training if they committed offenses such as not coming on time to the parade ground.

The boys were told that if the SPLA came to the area, they had to defend their cattle against the SPLA. After ten months of training the older boys in this group were taken to Mundri in Western Equatoria to fight against the SPLA. James was left behind to guard. Friends came back and told him that part of their group was killed in battle.

He and other boys were armed and taken back to their village to set up a militia post there. While in the village, he was able to see his family.

Four months later the Mundari militia collected three of the militia boys and took them back to Terekeka. They told them this was to give them military numbers so they would be "paid salaries as soldiers." James was one of the three. He and the other two spent another six months in Terekeka receiving military training from Mundari militia with government army officers. They trained many other boys with them, perhaps thirty to fifty. All the boys were Dinka.

They took this whole group of Dinka youngsters to Khartoum and from there to a large military training camp at the Jebel Aulia base some forty kilometers south of Khartoum. (The boys were promised they would be returned to their villages.) At Jebel Aulia they found many other recruits, more northerners than southerners.

James was at Jebel Aulia for several months, during which time he was paid 1,500 Sudanese pounds at the fifteenth day and 2,000 Sudanese pounds at the thirtieth day of the month. (A US dollar is now equivalent to 527 Sudanese pounds.)

In Jebel Aulia they were not beaten but they were proselytized. Army officers told them to become Muslims because "compared with Christianity, Islam is a good religion." They brought Muslims to talk to the trainees about Islam, but they did not bring any Christian priests or ministers to the military camp. James did not see a church at the camp but there was one mosque. The trainees were not threatened with punishment if they did not convert, however.

He and three others escaped together. At that time, James had been in the militia and in the military for about four years and he was no more than thirteen or fourteen.

Underage Recruitment from the Soba Street Boys' Camp

In late 1994, Dawa Islamiya took fifty-five boys from the Soba street boys camp in Khartoum in military trucks to El Muglad in Southern Kordofan, according to one of the boys who went. We summarize this testimony below. It appears from this testimony that Dawa and the camp authorities enticed the boys to take the trip by telling them they might find work in the oil fields in El Muglad. Instead the only alternatives available to them were to join the army at the base in El Muglad or to return to Khartoum. Thirty-three of the fifty-five joined the army at El Muglad, although most deserted within a few months because of the harsh conditions of training, according to one who chose not to enlist:

> When the boys in the Soba camp for street children heard of the possibility of finding work in the oil fields, they went willingly; for years Sudanese have traveled to the Gulf to work in oil fields there, returning with far more money than they could ever have earned at home.
>
> They transported the fifty-five Soba boys in military trucks to El Muglad. None of the boys found any work in El Muglad, according to a fourteen-year-old who went. The boys were told the work would not be available until the rainy season was over. (At that time of year, in October or November 1994, it could have been a month or more to the end of the rainy season.)
>
> After they were in El Muglad five days, Dawa Islamiya informed the boys that they had a choice: they could join the army at the army base in El Muglad if they wanted to, or go back to Khartoum. They could not stay in El Muglad unless they joined the army. This offer was made to our informant, who was about fourteen at the time, too young for military service under Sudanese law, which sets the minimum age at eighteen.
>
> Thirty-three of the fifty-five Soba boys joined the army at the military camp at El Muglad. Twenty-two of them decided not to join and were returned on the sixth day to Khartoum in the military truck.

> By mid-May 1995, some six or seven months later, most of the boys who had entered the military in El Muglad had decided they did not like it, and deserted. According to those who returned to visit their friends in Soba, only seven of the thirty-three Soba boys were still in the military camp.[100]

From this description of events, it appears that they dangled the prospect of oil field jobs before the boys to lure them to El Muglad. As there were no such jobs there, it appears that the real reason for taking the boys to El Muglad at that time was to put them into a military training camp. This was not forced on the boys, however, but it was much more likely that the boys would sign up for the military in El Muglad than in Khartoum.

"Ezekiel's" Story

A seventeen-year-old Christian student, Ezekiel (not his real name), was forcibly recruited without notice to his family and subjected by force to indoctrination in Islam. The army press ganged him and thirteen other boys at a swimming place on the Nile near Juba in January 1995. The boys were sent to Khartoum on a military plane the same afternoon, without any notice to their families. They and scores of other southern boys underwent harsh military training and received Islamic and political instruction telling them that the south was "backward" and it had to be "brought to the light" of Islam. They were beaten when they refused as Christians to convert. He managed to escape and told the following story:[101]

> Ezekiel was an intermediate school student in Juba and a member of the local Bari tribe. On January 6, 1995, after school and lunch at home, he went to the Nile to bathe. Three army soldiers came and asked him to get out of the water. They also called the rest of the boys swimming in the Nile out of the water, fourteen in all, and asked them where they worked. He and the others said they were students, but since they had gone swimming not all of them were carrying identity cards.
>
> The soldiers took them to the slaughter house near the Nile where a military truck was waiting for them; they told all fourteen to get

---

[100] Interview, Khartoum, May 9, 1995.

[101] Interview, Khartoum, May 19, 1995.

in the truck. They drove to the military barracks in Juba where the boys' names were recorded. Some did not give their real names because they were planning to escape.

The group was taken to the airport the same afternoon, without notice to their parents, and flown to Khartoum. All fourteen were sent off, even those with student identity cards.

They were dropped off at a military facility called the Southern Coordination Office for the Military, New Extension, Street 61, in Khartoum, where they fell asleep. They were wakened at 11 p.m. and driven to another military vehicle, which took them to a place outside Khartoum.

The next morning about 114 new boys joined them. They found out that the name of the place was Soba, and it was a military base.[102] In the afternoon another 130 southern boys were brought in.

They stayed three days in Soba and then 168 boys were taken at about 11 p.m. to an unknown place. (They found out there were 168 boys when their names were called while they were in formation on the parade grounds.) The name of the place, they learned, was "Disa," east of the Blue Nile in the direction of Damazien.

Ezekiel and the others started military training. Every morning when recruits' names were called at the parade ground, there were some missing: those who knew a route out were escaping.

During the two months before Ezekiel escaped, "many bad things happened" at the camp. The recruits were beaten daily with a whip or sticks, especially if they failed in military training.

During training the instructors would tell them they should become Muslims. Those who refused were beaten. All Ezekiel's Juba group refused because they were Christians. Because they refused, they were hit on the body and back with a whip.

---

[102] This is not to be confused with the Soba Camp for street boys.

Every morning at parade, the officers would ask those who had decided to become Muslims to raise their hands. Everyone stayed quiet, since all the recruits at this camp were Christians, except eleven Muslims who came from the Nuba Mountains.

After the evening meal they would ask the trainees to go to the barracks where a Muslim teacher and the eleven Muslim boys were studying the Koran. "Even if you are not a Muslim, just hear what we are going to say," they said. The boys decided to listen because if they refused they would be beaten.

There was no priest and no church at the military camp. They told the Christian recruits they could not pray on Sunday. Once the Christians went to pray on Sunday under a tree and were physically beaten. They could not openly sing Christian hymns; if they tried, they would be stopped. They were told that every Friday they should go for noonday Muslim prayers.

Their instructors told them the purpose of the war was to liberate the south from darkness. "And you who are in darkness can become Muslims and be brought to the light." The recruits were told they were being trained to become holy warriors (*mujahedeen*). Even if they died in *jihad* (holy war), they would go to Paradise.

They were told they were going to fight Garang, who was an outlaw, *kawarish*; the trainers cautioned that all southerners were rebels.

The recruits were warned that 1) if they fought as Christians and were killed, there would be no space in Paradise for them and 2) on earth (in the army) they would not be paid anything if they remained Christians. In fact, Ezekiel was never paid anything during the two months he was in the army.

The recruits slept on the floor inside long barracks and were given one blanket each. It was cold at night in January and February, "the coldest time in the coldest part of Sudan." They ate lentils mixed with ladyfinger broth (*bamiya*, a long green plant) but they never had enough food. They also ate sorghum porridge that was not properly cooked.

He befriended an older soldier who was not a northerner; he asked the man to show him the way to Khartoum and the soldier described how to get there from the base.

In February many soldiers went to Damazien for a holiday and the recruits were left alone with only a few guards. Ezekiel and five others from Juba escaped through the route described to him.

They walked hours, without food or water. They reached an Arab village and slept under a tree that night. It was cold but they could not go to any house because they were afraid of discovery. These southern boys were still wearing the clothes they were given for military training, white *damuria* (cotton).

At 3 a.m., they started moving again. They got to the road and found the bus stop for the bus from Damazien to Khartoum, which arrived at 10 a.m. They got on. They did not have any money for the fare.

One boy knew a southern soldier who was on the bus and "talked his language" and this soldier offered to pay the fare for three boys. Another southern woman on the bus offered to pay for the other three boys.

Meanwhile they discovered at the military camp that six had escaped. They sent a man from the base to intercept the bus at a certain location: he had the police stop the bus and search it. They caught the boys.

Some southern soldiers started a discussion with the other soldiers who wanted to take the boys back to the camp. They asked the boys their opinion. The boys told how they had been caught in Juba and brought to Khartoum the same afternoon without the knowledge of their families. They insisted they did not want to return to the military camp where they had been mistreated.

Because a large crowd gathered and heard this, the would-be captors withdrew and the boys were allowed to continue to Khartoum on the bus.

This was the first time any of them were in Khartoum. After getting on the wrong bus that went in the direction of a military base, they flagged down a southerner passing by in a car and he gave them a lift to Khartoum North. They stayed that night in the house of this Dinka man and in the morning he gave them a change of clothes and took them to the market where they finally found their relatives.

5
TREATMENT OF SPLA CHILD SOLDIERS BY THE GOVERNMENT OF SUDAN

This section addresses only two categories of young SPLA soldiers who have fallen into the hands of the government. We do not know what has happened to the majority of the SPLA child soldiers in the control of the government, just as we do not know the fate of the adult SPLA soldiers captured by the government. The government still refuses to permit the International Committee of the Red Cross to register and visit any detainees or prisoners whatsoever.

In 1992 the government of Sudan captured, amid much publicity, nineteen young SPLA soldiers who were too sick to be evacuated from Pochalla when it fell to the government. It took them to Khartoum where, after medical treatment, they were subjected to a brutal regime of Islamization enforced by beatings, failing to respect the freedom of religion of these children. In 1993, the government of Sudan encouraged a group of seven young SPLA soldiers, who had returned to Africa after being educated in Cuba, to return to Khartoum instead of to SPLA-controlled territory. As an inducement, the government promised them educational opportunities. The government failed to live up to its promises.

These two groups of child soldiers became more visible because the government chose to highlight their situation, for propaganda reasons. The government of Sudan has long tried to bring attention and condemnation to the SPLA's underage recruitment practices. Unfortunately, in dealing with groups of young SPLA soldiers, the government has not always lived up to its promises, and has pressured them to convert to Islam, which violates the boys' freedom of religion.

Pochalla Boy Soldiers

Pochalla, a town on the Sudanese side of the Ethiopian border, was the first stop for thousands of Sudanese refugees fleeing Ethiopia in May 1991. By the time Pochalla fell to the government army in 1992, almost all the refugees, including thousands of "unaccompanied minors," had already been evacuated by the SPLA. Some nineteen boys who were ill, and those caring for them, remained behind.

The Sudanese government army captured these nineteen, and seized upon them as evidence of SPLA mistreatment of children.[103] President Omar al-Bashir visited Pochalla to celebrate its capture, and he flew back to Khartoum with these boys

---

[103] Some government statements referred to the children, aged between eight and fifteen, as hostages. The boy interviewed referred to himself as a member of the SPLA. Reuter, "Sudan: Sudanese Leader Visits Recaptured Southern Town," Khartoum, March 19, 1992.

in tow. Although they were Christians, they were put into a Koranic school and lashed if they did not attend religious lessons. Many fled this ill-treatment and lack of respect for their freedom of religion, according to one of these boys whose testimony follows.[104]

> Domingo (not his real name) is a Dinka from Bahr El Ghazal. In 1987, when he was about ten, he joined an SPLA-organized mass exodus of boys seeking schooling in the refugee camps of Ethiopia, since the school system in southern Sudan, never very highly developed, had collapsed. His studies in Ethiopia were interrupted when he came down with smallpox.
>
> In 1991, after the fall of Mengistu, he left the Fugnido refugee camp in the mass exodus back to Sudan. "Ethiopia started to be bad, they were chasing us from Ethiopia so we went to Sudan." He was then about fourteen.
>
> In 1991-1992 he and over one hundred thousand Sudanese refugees were on the Ethiopia/Sudan border, near Pochalla.
>
> Most of the boys who had been separated from their families left in large SPLA-organized groups and many ultimately reached Kenya, but others remained behind because they were ill. He was one of nineteen sick boys who were in the clinic when the town was captured.
>
> Pochalla was attacked by the Ethiopian army and the SPLA resisted then withdrew from the town. Ethiopian troops came up to the health center where they boys were, but did not enter. After the battle, the Ethiopian army evacuated the nineteen boys from the clinic to the center of Pochalla, and Sudan government soldiers arrived. (The boys could tell the difference between Ethiopian and Sudanese soldiers because they had lived in Ethiopia for several years.)
>
> Lt. Gen. Omar al-Bashir, president of Sudan, visited Pochalla in a military plane to mark the return of Pochalla to government control.

---

[104] Interview, Khartoum, May 19, 1995.

He took the boys back to Khartoum with him on this plane, with some teachers. There was much fanfare about the boys, whom they had rescued. The boys were treated at the military hospital in Omdurman for the next month and a half.

Then they were taken to a Koranic school near Jebel Aulia, a military base about forty kilometers south of Khartoum. They stayed two months, living in a dormitory beside the school and mosque, but were not allowed to leave the compound.

Some slept on beds, others on the ground. They received two meals daily, only one bread at each meal, no meat, no milk. They did not have enough to eat. They were wakened at night to pray (Islamic prayers).

When they were captured, they were all Christians, but at the Islamic school in Jebel Aulia they were taught Arabic and the Koran. On the first day at this school the boys tried to refuse the Koranic teaching and were beaten for their refusal. The teacher lashed each of them ten times, so they agreed to comply and learn the Koran.

The nineteen boys were later moved to El Fau, between Wad Medani and Gedaref, to a Koranic school near Hanan village. At this school they received the same teaching as in Jebel Aulia: Arabic and the Koran. They did not receive any instruction in English, southern dialects or languages, or the Christian religion.

One day they all resisted learning the Koran. A southern man came and advised them not to resist so they would not be beaten. He told them "just to learn it. It would not stick."

From there they started to escape one by one, along with other boys from the Toposa tribe who had been captured when Kapoeta fell in May 1992 to the government. Some boys even escaped on buses sent to a market near this village to collect Christians to greet the Pope when he visited Khartoum in early 1993.

Since this time, the government has continued to denounce the SPLA's use of child soldiers.[105]

Unaccompanied SPLA Boy Soldiers from Cuba Disillusioned in Khartoum

Simon Mathiang Maker Kulong, who was born 1973 in Yirol, went to the refugee camps in Ethiopia and then to Cuba in 1986 under SPLA auspices when he was thirteen. He was trained in Cuba as a general medical technician, and returned to Uganda in 1993 with seven other Cuban-trained Sudanese boys who were to return to southern Sudan.[106] At this time, however, the SPLA faction fighting was at its height. This group conferred and decided they did not want to take sides in the faction fighting against other southerners, so they decided to go to government-controlled Sudan. The government promised they could continue their education in Khartoum and would receive other benefits.

The boys, whose return to Khartoum instead of to the SPLA was widely trumpeted by the government, did not realize any of the promises of education the government made them; some who have not fled the country but remain in Khartoum are bitter about the government's manipulation of them.[107]

The government nevertheless continues to seek the return of the rest of the young SPLA recruits from Cuba to Khartoum. Our source estimates their number at 275 boys and a government delegation that visited Cuba in June 1995 said there were 217.[108] The government recently noted that, "Interestingly enough, and sadly enough

---

[105] "The Crocodile Tears, Part II: No Future Without Honesty & Credibility: Inter-agencies' Response to Amnesty International," undated (1995), pp. 11-15. "The Crocodile Tears, Part I" was issued by the Sudan government. Part II was issued by government agencies and NGOs closely aligned with the government.

[106] Those unaccompanied boys trained in Cuba in civilian occupations realized the SPLA promise of education, unlike many others. *See* below.

[107] Interview, Khartoum, May 19, 1995.

[108] Reuter, "Sudan Seeks Return of 217 Children from Cuba," Khartoum, July 23, 1995. A government newspaper announced that Sudan would send a delegation to Cuba this week to seek the "release" of 217 children sent there by southern rebels.

too, now the returned children speak Spanish besides their mother tongue."[109] A summary of the testimony of Simon, the leader of the group, follows.

> Before he left Ethiopia for Cuba, Simon, who was only about thirteen, was given military training by the SPLA. Some 600 boys in all were taken to Cuba to continue their education.
>
> "Dr. John [Garang] said we had to study to build the New Sudan." Of the 600, an estimated 325 have since returned to Sudan, almost all to SPLA-controlled areas, and 275 are still studying in Cuba as of mid-1995. The government is eager to have them return to Khartoum instead of SPLA areas.
>
> Simon's group of seven returnees decided to return to the government-controlled areas instead of the SPLA-held south because at the time, in 1993, the two southern rebel factions were fighting each other. They did not want to have to take sides in this. Simon was the only Dinka in the group of seven; the rest were Nuer. "We talked it over. We would return and live as before." Some had family obligations in the north (to which their families had been displaced) as well.
>
> After these boys went to the UNHCR and said they wanted to return to Sudan (Khartoum), the Sudan Embassy in Kampala approached them. The government promised they could continue their studies in Khartoum, where there were twenty-four universities.
>
> "We returned to our country. They asked about the SPLA and we told them about building a New Sudan. The government then did not give us more information and our schooling was put off." The boys accused the government of lying to them about the schooling. The government apparently told the boys they had to work. Of the seven, four did not finish their studies and three have left the country.

---

[109] Sudan Information Office, Embassy of the Republic of Sudan, London, UK, press release of July 21, 1995.

The group found it hard to fit into the strict style of life in Khartoum after living in a Latin country that allows more individual freedom. They also complained of racial discrimination in Khartoum.

Since he was trained as a general medical assistant, the government assigned Simon to a hospital run by Dawa Islamiya, a large Islamic relief agency. The hospital director, however, asked him if he was a Muslim. Simon said "No, you can see by my name I am a Christian." This director made life difficult for him because he was not a Muslim, so Simon left work but returned when the director was removed for other reasons.

The boys say they relied on the government's promises when they decided to go to Khartoum instead of southern Sudan. They now believe they were lied to so that the government could use the boys' choice to score political points against the SPLA; when it accomplished that objective, the government lost interest in them and failed to live up to any promises.

PART II
UPDATE ON ABUSES BY THE REBELS

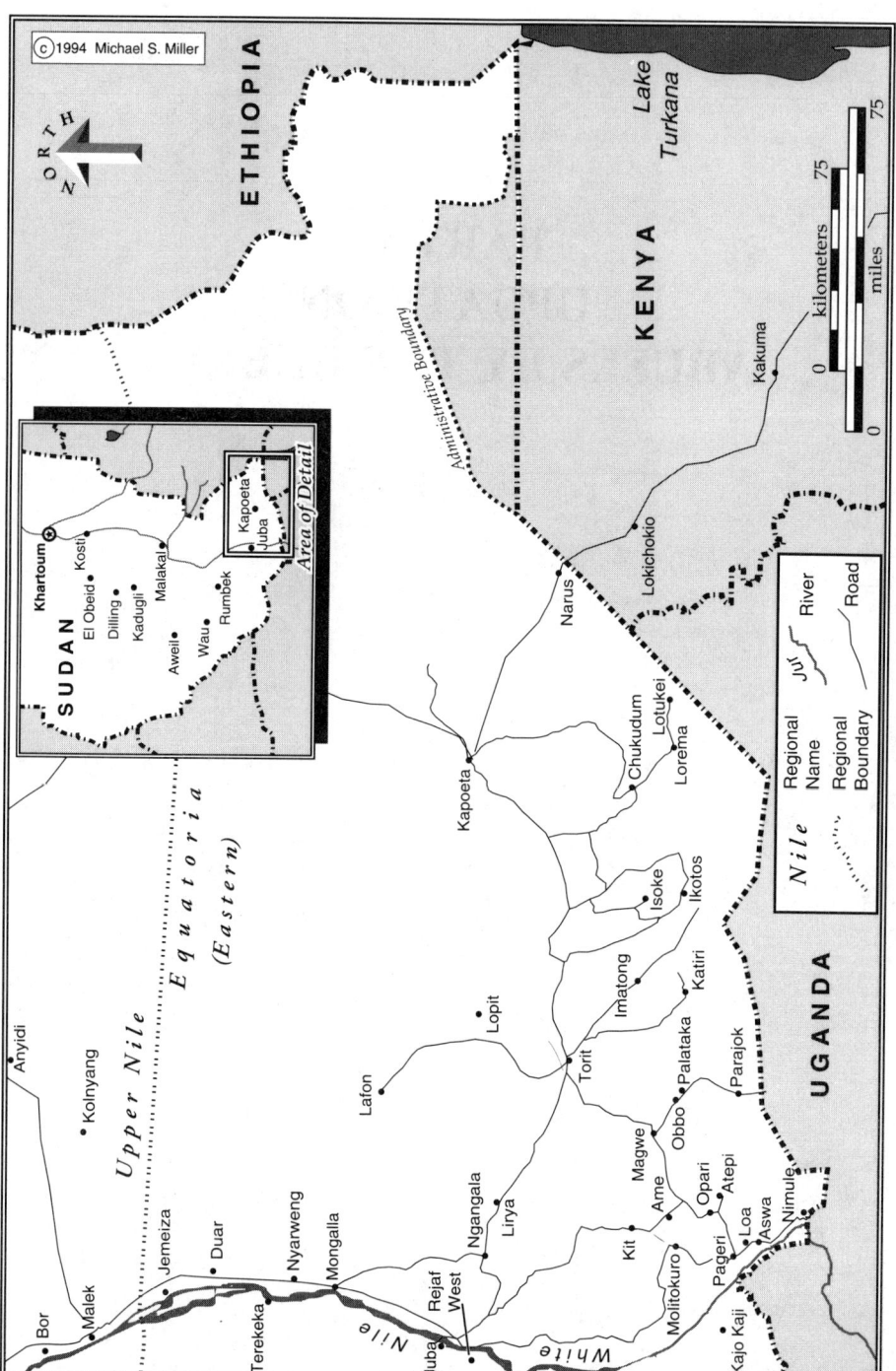

Eastern Equatoria

SOUTHERN SUDAN

As already described,[110] the SPLM/A and SSIM/A have engaged in warehousing young boys to hold them in preparation for military recruitment when needed. This began by encouraging and organizing boys to walk hundreds of kilometers to Ethiopian refugee camps in the mid-1980s, with the promise that they would receive an education there. This promise was attractive since the school system in southern Sudan had generally collapsed.

The primary purpose, however, of luring and keeping thousands of boys away from their families and in separate boys-only camps was, in the judgment of Human Rights Watch, a military purpose. This resulted in the training and recruitment of thousands of underage soldiers who were thrust into battle in southern Sudan and briefly in Ethiopia.

The Sudanese refugees deserted the Ethiopian refugee camps when the Ethiopian government fell in May 1991. Thousands of boys separated from their families but not yet incorporated into the SPLA arrived with the rest of the refugees in southern Sudan. In 1993 UNICEF began a project to reunify unaccompanied boys with their families, where both wanted reunification.

The SPLA never cooperated with UNICEF's family reunification program, and kept the boys in large groups close to SPLA military camps, and to call them up when needed. It also continued to recruit minors.

The SSIA cooperated with the UNICEF family reunification effort, but unfortunately did not stop underage recruitment. In 1993-94 it lured hundreds of boys from their homes in Upper Nile south to Eastern Equatoria, on the pretext that they would get schooling there. They actually received military training at the base of Cmdr. William Nyuon.

They received little food and no medical attention at the base, however. As their condition worsened Cmdr. Nyuon sent them to Lafon, the nearest U.N. relief site under the control of the SSIA, for medical aid and food; forty-seven unaccompanied boys died in Lafon between July and December 1994. Subsequently the SSIA cooperated in a UNICEF family reunification program that airlifted more than 780 unaccompanied boys from Lafon back to their homes in Upper Nile in 1994-95.

In the last three years, UNICEF has reunited more than 1,200 unaccompanied boys with their families. Some 4,500 known unaccompanied children

---

[110] Human Rights Watch/Africa and Children's Rights Project, "Sudan: The Lost Boys."

living in camps inside southern Sudan have yet to be reunified, according to UNICEF.[111]

---

[111] OLS Southern Sector, Press Release, "Southern Sudanese Celebrate Day of the African Child," Nairobi, Kenya, June 14, 1995.

6
SOUTHERN SUDAN INDEPENDENCE MOVEMENT/ARMY

In 1993-94 the SSIA lured hundreds of Nuer boys from the Ler area of Upper Nile province to Lafon, Eastern Equatoria, hundreds of kilometers to the south. The SSIA had told the boys that there were schools and education in Lafon, and they promised them that they could attend school there. So great is the demand by southerners and their children for education that the boys were permitted to leave home.

The boys did not go directly to Lafon but ended up in a boys' camp next to the military camp of Cmdr. William Nyuon Bany in Magire, Eastern Equatoria. Cmdr. Nyuon, who spent most of his time attacking the SPLA forces in Eastern Equatoria, apparently asked Cmdr. Riek for additional troops in late 1993, which was part if not all the reason for the disguised recruitment drive around Ler. Cmdr. William Nyuon, a Nuer, was in the SPLA until September 1992, when he defected to join the forces of Cmdr. Riek Machar Terry Dhurgon, who had formed his own faction in August 1991, now known as SSIM/A. In September 1992 Cmdr. Nyuon and his troops fled SPLA headquarters in Pageri, close to the Triple A displaced camps south of Juba.[112] SPLA forces pursued him. Cmdr. Nyuon's troops made it to Lafon in October 1992 and Cmdr. Riek's forces moved down from Upper Nile to reinforce him that same month. SPLA forces followed and there were several encounters in and around Lafon in the following months. SPLA forces occupied Lafon in February 1993 and pulled out in April 1993, when Nyuon's forces reentered, keeping a base at Magire near Juba.

As on the earlier journeys from Upper Nile east to Ethiopian refugee camps in the mid-1980s, the trips 1993-94 south were on foot and took at least a month. The boys traveled in several different groups that departed over a period of months or perhaps a year. Some were said to have been transported in vehicles supplied to Cmdr. Nyuon by the Sudan government, in an arrangement that united enemies of the SPLA.

The hazards of the trip included attacks by SPLA forces as Nuer children passed through Dinka or SPLA territory. One group of boys traveling from Ler in Upper Nile left in November 1993; Cmdr. Nyuon's forces escorted this group (including some women and small children). At Yom Ciir, an SPLA-controlled village north of Juba, the SPLA attacked the column in November-December 1993 and caused great loss of life.

One boy then about nine years old who was part of that group said that he left home with many boys and men in late 1993. They traveled one month to Ayod

---

[112] The Triple A camps were so called because they were located in Asthma, Atepi and Ame; together they housed an estimated 100,000 displaced persons.

southwest of Nasir and then on to Lafon. On the way, they were "attacked by Dinka. It was very heavy and people died. I will never forget it," this boy said in a whisper.

Cmdr. Nyuon gave the boys military training in Magire, at least two months of training in 1994 (according to one source this took place between April and June 1994). Approximately 80 percent of these boys were under fifteen years of age, according to a survey made after they were in Lafon.

Cmdr. Nyuon was not able to feed them enough so some fell ill. They were dependent for their food on the government of Sudan, with which Cmdr. Nyuon had an agreement for some logistical and materiel support to enable him to attack the SPLA, their common enemy. The support he received from the government of Sudan was not enough, however. Boys later told social workers that "the Arabs did not give us much food." Apparently the Lord's Resistance Army (LRA), a Ugandan rebel (Christian fundamentalist) group receiving substantial assistance from the government of Sudan, brought food in military trucks to Magire occasionally. There was little or no medical attention at this camp, and some boys died for lack of medical care, according to one familiar with the situation.

When the condition of the new recruits seriously worsened, Cmdr. Nyuon started sending them, with an escort, to nearby Lafon for food and medicine, beginning in June or July 1994. The SSIA forces were then in control of Lafon, where there was a large civilian population of the Pari tribe[113] and an international relief program for these civilians. After the first large group of boys arrived in Lafon from Magire, others continued to be sent by Cmdr. Nyuon to Lafon in smaller groups; sick boys were of no use to any military commander.[114]

Also reaching Lafon were Nuer civilians, including unaccompanied boys, who fled Atepi displaced persons camp when Cmdr. Nyuon defected from the SPLA in September 1992. Included in this group were some who had been to Ethiopia and back. We summarize their testimonies below.

"Kuech's" Story

One youngster who did not know his age, Kuech (not his real name), was born near Ler. He made the long journey on foot to Itang refugee camp in Ethiopia for an education in 1988 with other boys. He finished the fifth level of study in Nuer and studied the first level of English before evacuating Itang in 1991. He and a

---

[113] *See*, "Eisei Kurimoto," Civil War and Regional Conflict: The Pari and Their Neighbors in Southeastern Sudan," in Katsuyoshi Fukui and John Markakis, ed. *Ethnicity and Conflict in the Horn of Africa* (James Currey, London: 1994), pp. 95 *et seq.*

[114] Interview, Lokichokio, Kenya, March 13, 1995.

large group of boys traveled to Magire, where they stayed "very close" to the military camp of Cmdr. Nyuon in Magire. According to him, they spent their time farming, mostly planting okra, and they had no school and no military training. Finally in 1994 Nyuon provided an escort to Lafon, where they attended school for four months before returning to Ler in the 1995 UNICEF airlift. [115]

"William's" Story
William (not his real name), born in 1981 in Ler, had five brothers and four sisters. He made the journey to Itang in 1989, when he was eight, without his family but in the company of many other boys, in search of an education. In the Fugnido refugee camp school he finished the first level in English and the fourth level in Nuer. Fleeing Ethiopia in 1991, he walked with others to Pochalla, Pibor, Bor, Lirya (from which they were driven by the "Arabs"), Torit (four months, where there was a school), and Atepi. He said, "people were deceiving us that there was a school in Lirya so we went there and there was no school." After spending five months in Atepi, he and others left partly because there was no school there, "not even for Dinka," but mostly because Cmdr. Nyuon, a Nuer, defected from Garang and the Nuer in Atepi displaced persons camp were "afraid that the Dinka would kill the Nuer" as a result. They left the same day they heard of Cmdr. Nyuon's defection in September 1992. [116]

"Peter's" Story
Peter (not his real name), a Nuer boy born about 1983 in the Nuyong district of Nial, Upper Nile, went to Itang in 1990 with his mother and siblings (he was a middle child of eight); his father had died. He was studying in Fugnido refugee camp but "When we were trying to learn the alphabet, we had to run away." With his family, he fled to Pochalla and made a trek similar to the one described above; on the way to Isoke his grandmother was shot dead by robbers. He fled Atepi for Lafon after Cmdr. William Nyuon's defection from the SPLA, and arrived in Lafon on

---

[115] Interview, Ler, Upper Nile, Sudan, March 13, 1995.

[116] Interview, Ler, Upper Nile, Sudan, March 13, 1995.

December 30, 1992, shortly before Lafon was attacked by Garang's SPLA forces. They and the original residents of Lafon, the Pari, fled outside Lafon and stayed there until the SPLA left several months later. He came down with malaria and his brother contracted Kala Azar[117] in Lafon, but he was able to go to school for four months in 1993 in Lafon, the first schooling he had since 1991. He finished the fourth level of Nuer and in December 1994 was evacuated to Ler. [118]

By September 1994 there were more than 600 unaccompanied boys in Lafon, who arrived in the ways described below. There were teachers and a working school at that time, although it had only been open for a few months. CARE was providing primary health care. Norwegian Church Aid, which had a program ten years ago in Lafon, was engaged in teacher training of forty teachers in Lafon, including Pari teachers for the indigenous population. Because of the security situation in Lafon,[119] however, the teacher training program could not be completed.[120] While there was some education at Lafon, it was far from what the boys had been promised. One eleven-year-old said he thought that they would be taught English (in contrast to the Nuer dialect) in Lafon, but there was no school in Lafon while he was there. [121]

Even after arriving in Lafon, the boys did not receive the care and attention they required. Although there was a feeding center set up for them in Lafon in July 1994, and their health improved, by November it had dramatically worsened again and many died. Knowledgeable sources attributed this to continuing theft of the boys' food

---

[117] Kala Azar is visceral Leishmaniasis, a parasitic disease. Kala Azar means "black fever." Its symptoms include fever, diarrhea, and coughing, and in the advanced stage, hyper pigmentation of the skin (hence the name "black fever"). Left untreated, in children 75 to 85 percent will die, and in adults 90 to 95 percent will die within a course of three to twenty months.

[118] Interview, Ler, Upper Nile, Sudan, March 13, 1995.

[119] Lafon has changed hands several times during the war on account of its strategic location. See Human Rights Watch/Africa, *Civilian Devastation*, pp. 136-41. In 1994 and 1995 misconduct by SSIA forces caused the Pari to withdraw their allegiance from the SSIA, although they never returned to the government fold.

[120] Interview, Lokiochokio, Kenya, March 13, 1995.

[121] Interview, Ler, Upper Nile, Sudan, March 13, 1995.

rations by the SSIA soldiers and others, and to other reasons. The forty-seven deaths of unaccompanied boys between July and December 1994 in Lafon would not have occurred if the boys had received the food and medical attention intended for them.

This is a graphic illustration of the difficulties of protecting unaccompanied boys, even in sites regularly visited by U.N. relief personnel. As long as they remain scattered around southern Sudan, they will remain prey to abuse and to recruitment into the military, one source concluded; they are also likely to be manipulated and abused to attract food and other aid to locations where the military may benefit. Another source believes that the boys were denied food in order to attract more relief to the area, in other words, that they were used as "bait," and the situation got out of hand.

When matters came to a head with so many deaths, UNICEF asked for and received the cooperation of the SSIA to send the boys back to their families. In December 7-9, 1994, 495 boys were airlifted to Ler. The U.N. decided to go ahead with the program even if all the children were not well, since some twenty-two died in Lafon between November and December 1994.[122] Some had to be hospitalized in Ler on arrival.[123]

Even during this evacuation of the boys, there were problems with local SSIA commanders who were loath to see potential young recruits being taken away. Even as about 600 boys were lined up to get on the UNICEF/OLS plane that was to take them to Ler, one of the local SSIA commanders, Gathoth Gatwic Gatkouth,[124] went down the line and took out the boys he thought most fit, about one hundred in all. When UNICEF personnel protested, he said, "'These are strong and they can help us.'"

After a complaint was lodged with Cmdr. Riek, this commander was dismissed the following month, and he defected to Cmdr. Nyuon, based in Magire.[125] Some boys picked out of the line to board the plane in December 1994 got sick in

---

[122] Operation Lifeline Sudan (OLS) Southern Sector, "Update, 13 December 1994," Nairobi, Kenya, p. 1.

[123] In Ler ten were admitted to hospital for kala azar, tuberculosis, skin and chest infections, hepatitis and diarrhea. OLS Southern Sector "Update, 20 December 1994," p. 1.

[124] He was also alleged to have recruited many of the boys from their homes in Upper Nile in 1993-94.

[125] By this time, February 1995, Cmdr. Nyuon had been expelled by Cmdr. Riek from the SSIA. Since then, Cmdr. Nyuon rejoined the SSIM/A, the SPLM/A and the SSIM/A have come to an agreement on a cease-fire, and the accommodation between the Sudan government and Cmdr. Nyuon seems to have ended.

Magire from the usual causes, lack of food and medicine, and were sent back to Lafon in 1995.

In late January 1995, a U.N. team visited Lafon and learned that there were still some 300 boys in Lafon and Magire. These may have been brought from other locations. Cmdr. Nyuon asked that they and some 500 women and children displaced (mostly Nuers) be relocated to their places of origin in Upper Nile.[126]

On March 13 and 19, 1995, some 133 boys, 259 women and children, and thirty-seven teachers and disabled were flown from Lafon to Ler, Ayod, Duar, Nasir and Waat in Upper Nile by UNICEF.[127]

As with the government's continuing capture of street children while at the same time it embarks on a family reunification program of other street children, the SSIM/A's two-faced policy threatens to make a revolving door of the UNICEF family reunification program.

Meanwhile, other groups of youth, long since separated from their families by SPLA military/education policies, are still scattered about Sudan. A mostly Nuba group of boys, about 600, fled Nasir because of fighting between Nuer sections in May 1994. They were temporarily relocated in Malual and then were moved to Maiwut north of Jokau in June 1994,[128] all in Upper Nile territory nominally under the control of the SSIA.

A headcount in Maiwut in December 1994 showed there were some 1,185 unaccompanied boys there. When the Sudan government refused flight clearance for Maiwut in January 1995, these boys and the 10,900 displaced persons in Maiwut were placed in jeopardy.[129]

A headcount in January 1995 showed that the Maiwut boys dropped in number from 1,188 to 488; about 450 of them, mostly Nuba, moved to Pagak, thirty kilometers north, where there was a better supply of water.[130] Pagak was the only accessible area in eastern Upper Nile since relief workers were evacuated from Nasir

---

[126] OLS Southern Sector, "Update, 31 January 1995."

[127] OLS Southern Sector, Press Release, "Humanitarian Emergency feared in northern Bahr El Ghazal," Nairobi, Kenya, March 21, 1995.

[128] OLS Southern Sector, "Weekly Update, 7 June 1994," p. 1.

[129] OLS Southern Sector, "Monthly Report, December 1994," p. 7, Nairobi, Kenya.

[130] OLS Southern Sector, "Monthly Report, January 1995," p.9.

in February 1995;[131] Nasir fell to the government in March 1995. The Sudan government refused flight clearances to Pagak in May 1995, and continued to refuse clearances to Maiwut.[132] By the end of June 1995 there were only 200 unaccompanied boys left in Maiwut, an area still inaccessible due to insecurity.[133]

Most sought help in Ethiopia. Some 240 Nuba, 287 Nuer, 175 Dinka, and nine others, a total of 711 unaccompanied boys, were registered in 1995 as new refugees by the UNHCR at Fugnido refugee camp in Ethiopia by June, according to a social worker. By August the total unaccompanied minor population in Fugnido was 1,235, including those registered in prior years.[134]

The Sudan government consulate in Gambella, Ethiopia, visited the refugee camps on several occasions, trying to encourage the refugees to repatriate. One source said they were particularly focusing on the Nuba boys. The Sudan government steadfastly refuses humanitarian access in the Nuba Mountains except to garrison towns. It is not possible to conduct a family reunification program for the Nuba boys to the nongovernment areas of the Nuba Mountains, as has been done with the Nuer boys to nongovernment areas of Upper Nile. Nor is it feasible, for security reasons, for the Nuba boys to return home on their own.

The refugees, who have adamantly refused to return to Sudan although asked to by the Sudan government, were supported by the Ethiopian government and its refugee agency (and presence of its army), so that any "irregular interference" with the refugees such as forced conscription has been reduced.[135]

---

[131] OLS Southern Sector, "Monthly Report, April 1995," p. 9.

[132] OLS Southern Sector, "Update, 2 May 1995."

[133] OLS Southern Sector, "Monthly Report, June 1995," p. 11.

[134] Fax, UNCHR, Addis Ababa, to Human Rights Watch, New York, August 9, 1995. A majority of the 1,235 (or about 800 boys, some 66 percent) are Nuer. No other tribal breakdown was available.

[135] Ibid.

7
SUDAN PEOPLE'S LIBERATION MOVEMENT/ARMY

The SPLM/A has never permitted any family reunification program to operate in its jurisdiction. Most unaccompanied minors who came from Ethiopia in 1991 and remain in its territory by now either have been absorbed by the SPLA as combatants or fled to Kakuma, a refugee camp in northern Kenya.

There were more than 10,000 unaccompanied boys at Kakuma when the camp opened in 1992: their numbers decreased to 7,524[136] as of March 1995.[137]

We received reports that the SPLA has continued to recruit young boys in 1994 and 1995. The SPLA, like the government, seems short of recruits all the time. Many SPLA soldiers came and continue to come from Bahr El Ghazal. However, it takes about three months to make the journey from Bahr El Ghazal to the very south of Sudan. The need at the time was greatest for SPLA troops near the Uganda border Nimule because the government of Sudan is trying to push the SPLA from that front line into Uganda.[138]

Cmdr. Kuol Manyang, a top SPLA commander, said that it was their intention that "everyone should join in the armed struggle."[139] He maintained, however, that they do not recruit underage boys, because "they are not useful as soldiers." Cmdr. Kuol Manyang repeated that it is the policy of the SPLA to recruit only those who are eighteen and older, and to recruit them by enlightening them about why they should fight.

He admitted, however, that they give military training to boys fifteen and over. The boys are not taken at age fourteen or younger because they are too small and they do not know what they are doing. When the SPLA makes a mistake and takes

---

[136] This number consists of 3,770 unaccompanied boys in interim group care; 1,877 under foster care; and 1,877 united with friends or relatives, according to the UNHCR.

[137] The age distribution of the boys (estimated) at the end of 1994, when there were 2,700 boys in the interim group care at Kakuma, was as follows: 10 years: 10; 11 years: 18; 12 years: 127; 13 years: 326; 14 years: 754; 15 years: 1,103; 16 years: 1,023; 17 years: 952; 18 and over: 1,186. Those now eighteen years old were only fifteen when they arrived in Kenya in 1992. Interview, Kakuma, Kenya, March 17, 1995.

[138] Interview, Lokiochokio, Kenya, March 13, 1995. In August 1995, the government succeeded in breaking through to the Sudan border town of Kaya.

[139] Interview, Cmdr. Kuol Manyang Juuk, SPLA, March 16, 1995.

someone fourteen years old because he looks older, they release him when the parents tell them the boy is below age fifteen.[140]

Of course, boys kept in age-segregated camps far away from their families have no one who can defend them and no one who can verify their age. With no families around to make a fuss, inducting groups of underage boys into military service is easy.

Despite the disclaimers about the uselessness of underage boys, social workers familiar with this problem observed that the SPLA and SSIA seem to prefer boys to older recruits: using propaganda with them is easier, and their youth and strength are desirable.[141]

Relief officials have programs in Kakuma refugee camp for the estimated 3,200 boys there. Among other things, social workers now include in group discussions the notion that the boys are not obliged to join the military struggle; it is their choice. Apparently part of this message has gotten through to the boys. Cmdr. Kuol Manyang commented sarcastically, "Most in the refugee camps do not want military training. They prefer that their country be taken by the enemy, they do not mind."[142]

Nevertheless, a civilian allied with the SPLA reportedly used emotional ethnic appeals in 1994 to boys, "Let us take back our land from the Nuers," to persuade some 700 Dinka boys to voluntarily join.

Those boys still in southern Sudan, under the jurisdiction of the SPLA and far from the protection of the UNHCR, do not appear to have as much choice. The SPLA moved several thousand unaccompanied boys, some as young as seven (who lived in the abandoned compound of the Catholic Church in Palataka in 1993),[143] to Omere in March 1994. This was done to protect the boys because the Sudan government army started shelling the area. About 2,000 unaccompanied boys were reported to have made the move to Omere.[144] According to NGOs who saw them, many were at a cattle camp in Omere and therefore were not in bad health, because of

---

[140] Ibid.

[141] Interview, Lokiochokio, March 13, 1995.

[142] Interview, Cmdr. Kuol Manyang Juuk, SPLA, March 16, 1995.

[143] *See* Human Rights Watch, "Sudan, the Lost Boys."

[144] Interview, Labone, Eastern Equatoria, Sudan, March 15, 1995.

access to milk. However, the SPLA required them to do portering, and beat them when they refused, according to an eyewitness.[145]

When the Lord's Resistance Army and Sudan army troops attacked Labone[146] south of Parajok in March 1995, they attacked through Omere, causing the boys to flee. After the attack, the SPLA relocated the boys from Omere to the Labone displaced persons camp. By then, it appeared that there were only 200 boys left in the group; it was likely that the rest had been impressed into active military service.

Boys who are grouped together in other locations appear to be inducted on a continuing basis. Although there were 2,800 unaccompanied boys in Natinga in August 1994,[147] where there was a school for them, the director admitted to U.N. personnel in early March 1995 that there were only 600 boys left.[148] Since the destination of the others was left unstated and no request made for their relief, it may be assumed that they had been recruited. By June, the unaccompanied boys at Natinga had risen to 1,700.[149] It is not known how many of the additional boys were relocated from other places in southern Sudan such as Labone, and how many are new recruits.

The SPLA child soldiers grow up to be adult soldiers, having spent their youth in combat. Human Rights Watch/Africa met some of them. They included:

- a twenty-four-year-old soldier who had been in the SPLA since 1984, which means he joined at age fourteen; a Murle, he said he joined because "I wanted to fight for freedom for south Sudan;"

- a Nuer born in Waat who had been fighting for ten years; he is now twenty-five, so he was fifteen when he joined;

- a seventeen-year-old Dinka from Rumbek who has been a soldier for seven years, which means he joined at age ten; he studied in Dima refugee camp

---

[145] Interview, Labone, Eastern Equatoria, Sudan, March 14, 1995.

[146] Labone is one of the locations to which the displaced persons living in the Triple A camps were relocated in early 1994 in the face of a government offensive.

[147] OLS Southern Sector, "Monthly Report, August 1994," p. 6.

[148] Interview, Lokichokio, Kenya, March 16, 1995.

[149] OLS Southern Sector, Press Release, "Southern Sudanese Celebrate Day of the African Child," June 14, 1995.

in Ethiopia but considers that he has been a soldier since his arrival in Dima in 1987;

- a twenty-year-old Dinka from Aweil who went to Ethiopia in 1989 to join the SPLA; he was fourteen when he joined. He received primary school education in the Dima refugee camp as well as military training;
- a twenty-year-old Dinka from Gogrial, Bahr El Ghazal, left to join the SPLA when he was thirteen. He was among the boys at Natinga, where there was a school he attended for three years before becoming a full-time combatant; and
- a twenty-three-year-old Dinka from Aweil, who has never been to school, joined the SPLA by going to Ethiopia in 1985, when he was thirteen.[150]

None of these young men have seen their families since they joined the SPLA.

---

[150] Interviews, Kenya, March 18, 1995.

8
CONCLUSION

The children of Sudan, north and south, have been denied their basic rights by all parties to the conflict, and by the government of Sudan even in areas where there is no conflict going on. Those considered street children, mostly southerners and Nuba, are removed from their families without notice, denied their right to identity when they are given new Arab names, and denied their right to freedom of religion when they are subjected to forcible conversion. Dinka and Nuba children have been captured in military raids on their villages and taken into household slavery by their captors, with no government intervention to stop the practice and punish those who treat them as slaves. Underage boys are forcibly recruited into the army or militias by the government, which at the same time attempts to focus world attention on the SPLA's use of child soldiers.

The SSIA cooperates with UNICEF family reunification programs while at the same time it continues to recruit underage soldiers. In 1994, this practice lead to the deaths from malnutrition and illness of forty-seven unaccompanied boys. The SPLA has never permitted any family reunification programs within its jurisdiction and continues to induct underage boys.

APPENDIX
THE CONVENTION ON THE RIGHTS OF THE CHILD

Adopted by the United Nations General Assembly on 20 November 1989.
Entered into force on 2 September 1990 in accordance with article 49 (1).

PREAMBLE

The States Parties to the present Convention,
Considering that, in accordance with the principles proclaimed in the Charter of the United Nations, recognition of the inherent dignity and of the equal and inalienable rights of all members of the human family is the foundation of freedom, justice and peace in the world,

Bearing in mind that the peoples of the United Nations have, in the Charter, reaffirmed their faith in fundamental human rights and in the dignity and worth of the human person, and have determined to promote social progress and better standards of life in larger freedom,

Recognizing that the United Nations has, in the Universal Declaration of Human Rights and in the International Covenants on Human Rights, proclaimed and agreed that everyone is entitled to all the rights and freedoms set forth therein, without distinction of any kind, such as race, colour, sex, language, religion, political or other opinion, national or social origin, property,
birth or other status,

Recalling that, in the Universal Declaration of Human Rights, the United Nations has proclaimed that childhood is entitled to special care and assistance,

Convinced that the family, as the fundamental group of society and the natural environment for the growth and well-being of all its members and particularly children, should be afforded the necessary protection and assistance so that it can fully assume its responsibilities within the community,

Recognizing that the child, for the full and harmonious development of his or her personality, should grow up in a family environment, in an atmosphere of happiness, love and understanding,

Considering that the child should be fully prepared to live an individual life in society, and brought up in the spirit of the ideals proclaimed in the Charter of the United Nations, and in particular in the spirit of peace, dignity, tolerance, freedom, equality and solidarity,

Bearing in mind that the need to extend particular care to the child has been stated in the Geneva Declaration of the Rights of the Child of 1924 and in the Declaration of the Rights of the Child adopted by the General Assembly on 20 November 1959 and recognized in the Universal Declaration of Human Rights, in the International Covenant on Civil and Political Rights (in particular in articles 23 and 24), in the International Covenant on Economic, Social and Cultural Rights (in particular in article 10) and in the statutes and relevant instruments of specialized agencies and international organizations concerned with the welfare of children,

Bearing in mind that, as indicated in the Declaration of the Rights of the Child, "the child, by reason of his physical and mental immaturity, needs special safeguards and care, including appropriate legal protection, before as well as after birth,"

Recalling the provisions of the Declaration on Social and Legal Principles relating to the Protection and Welfare of Children, with Special Reference to Foster Placement and Adoption Nationally and Internationally; the United Nations Standard Minimum Rules for the Administration of Juvenile Justice (The Beijing Rules); and the Declaration on the Protection of Women and Children in Emergency and Armed Conflict,

Recognizing that, in all countries in the world, there are children living in exceptionally difficult conditions, and that such children need special consideration,

Taking due account of the importance of the traditions and cultural values of each people for the protection and harmonious development of the child,

Recognizing the importance of international co-operation for improving the living conditions of children in every country, in particular in the developing countries,

Have agreed as follows:

PART I

Article 1
For the purposes of the present Convention, a child means every human being below the age of eighteen years unless, under the law applicable to the child, majority is attained earlier.

Article 2
1. States Parties shall respect and ensure the rights set forth in the present Convention to each child within their jurisdiction without discrimination of any kind, irrespective of the child's or his or her parent's or legal guardian's race, colour, sex, language, religion, political or other opinion, national, ethnic or social origin, property, disability, birth or other status.

2. States Parties shall take all appropriate measures to ensure that the child is protected against all forms of discrimination or punishment on the basis of the status, activities, expressed opinions, or beliefs of the child's parents, legal guardians, or family members.

Article 3
1. In all actions concerning children, whether undertaken by public or private social welfare institutions, courts of law, administrative authorities or legislative bodies, the best interests of the child shall be a primary consideration.

2. States Parties undertake to ensure the child such protection and care as is necessary for his or her well-being, taking into account the rights and duties of his or her parents, legal guardians, or other individuals legally responsible for him or her, and, to this end, shall take all appropriate legislative and administrative measures.

3. States Parties shall ensure that the institutions, services and facilities responsible for the care or protection of children shall conform with the standards established by competent authorities, particularly in the areas of safety, health, in the number and suitability of their staff, as well as competent supervision.

Article 4
States Parties shall undertake all appropriate legislative, administrative, and other measures for the implementation of the rights recognized in the present Convention. With regard to economic, social and cultural rights, States Parties shall undertake such measures to the maximum extent of their available resources and, where needed, within the framework of international co-operation.

Article 5
States Parties shall respect the responsibilities, rights and duties of parents or, where applicable, the members of the extended family or community as provided for by local custom, legal guardians or other persons legally responsible for the child, to provide, in a manner consistent with the evolving capacities of the child, appropriate direction and guidance in the exercise by the child of the rights recognized in the present Convention.

Article 6
1. States Parties recognize that every child has the inherent right to life.

2. States Parties shall ensure to the maximum extent possible the survival and development of the child.

Article 7
1. The child shall be registered immediately after birth and shall have the right from birth to a name, the right to acquire a nationality and, as far as possible, the right to know and be cared for by his or her parents.

2. States Parties shall ensure the implementation of these rights in accordance with their national law and their obligations under the relevant international instruments in this field, in particular where the child would otherwise be stateless.

Article 8
1. States Parties undertake to respect the right of the child to preserve his or her identity, including nationality, name and family relations as recognized by law without unlawful interference.

2. Where a child is illegally deprived of some or all of the elements of his or her identity, States Parties shall provide appropriate assistance and protection, with a view to speedily re-establishing his or her identity.

Article 9
1. States Parties shall ensure that a child shall not be separated from his or her parents against their will, except when competent authorities subject to judicial review determine, in accordance with applicable law and procedures, that such separation is necessary for the best interests of the child. Such determination may be necessary in a particular case such as one involving abuse or neglect of the child by the parents, or one where the parents are living separately and a decision must be made as to the child's place of residence.

2. In any proceedings pursuant to paragraph 1 of the present article, all interested parties shall be given an opportunity to participate in the proceedings and make their views known.

3. States Parties shall respect the right of the child who is separated from one or both parents to maintain personal relations and direct contact with both parents on a regular basis, except if it is contrary to the child's best interests.

4. Where such separation results from any action initiated by a State Party, such as the detention, imprisonment, exile, deportation or death (including death arising from any cause while the person is in the custody of the State) of one or both parents or of the child, that State Party shall, upon request, provide the parents, the child or, if appropriate, another member of the family with the essential information concerning the whereabouts of the absent member(s) of the family unless the provision of the information would be detrimental to the well-being of the child. States Parties shall further ensure that the submission of such a request shall of itself entail no adverse consequences for the person(s) concerned.

Article 10
1. In accordance with the obligation of States Parties under article 9, paragraph 1, applications by a child or his or her parents to enter or leave a State Party for the purpose of family reunification shall be dealt with by States Parties in a positive, humane and expeditious manner. States Parties shall further ensure that the submission of such a request shall entail no adverse consequences for the applicants and for the members of their family.

2. A child whose parents reside in different States shall have the right to maintain on a regular basis, save in exceptional circumstances, personal relations and direct contacts with both parents. Towards that end and in accordance with the obligation of States Parties under article 9, paragraph 1, States Parties shall respect the right of the child and his or her parents to leave any country, including their own, and to enter their own country. The right to leave any country shall be subject only to such restrictions as are prescribed by law and which are necessary to protect the national security, public order (order public), public health or morals or the rights and freedoms of others and are consistent with the other rights recognized in the present Convention.

Article 11
1. States Parties shall take measures to combat the illicit transfer and non-return of children abroad.

2. To this end, States Parties shall promote the conclusion of bilateral or multilateral agreements or accession to existing agreements.

Article 12
1. States Parties shall assure to the child who is capable of forming his or her own views the right to express those views freely in all matters affecting the child, the views of the child being given due weight in accordance with the age and maturity of the child.

2. For this purpose, the child shall in particular be provided the opportunity to be heard in any judicial and administrative proceedings affecting the child, either directly, or through a representative or an appropriate body, in a manner consistent with the procedural rules of national law.

Article 13
1. The child shall have the right to freedom of expression; this right shall include freedom to seek, receive and impart information and ideas of all kinds, regardless of frontiers, either orally, in writing or in print, in the form of art, or through any other media of the child's choice.

2. The exercise of this right may be subject to certain restrictions, but these shall only be such as are provided by law and are necessary:

(a) For respect of the rights or reputations of others; or

(b) For the protection of national security or of public order (order public), or of public health or morals.

Article 14
1. States Parties shall respect the right of the child to freedom of thought, conscience and religion.

2. States Parties shall respect the rights and duties of the parents and, when applicable, legal guardians, to provide direction to the child in the exercise of his or her right in a manner consistent with the evolving capacities of the child.

3. Freedom to manifest one's religion or beliefs may be subject only to such limitations as are prescribed by law and are necessary to protect public safety, order, health or morals, or the fundamental rights and freedoms of others.

Article 15
1. States Parties recognize the rights of the child to freedom of association and to freedom of peaceful assembly.

2. No restrictions may be placed on the exercise of these rights other than those imposed in conformity with the law and which are necessary in a democratic society in the interests of national security or public safety, public order (order public), the protection of public health or morals or the protection of the rights and freedoms of others.

Article 16
1. No child shall be subjected to arbitrary or unlawful interference with his or her privacy, family, home or correspondence, nor to unlawful attacks on his or her honour and reputation.

2. The child has the right to the protection of the law against such interference or attacks.

Article 17
States Parties recognize the important function performed by the mass media and shall ensure that the child has access to information and material from a diversity of national and international sources, especially those aim edat the promotion of his or her social, spiritual and moral well-being and physical and mental health. To this end, States Parties shall:

(a) Encourage the mass media to disseminate information and material of social and cultural benefit to the child and in accordance with the spirit of article 29;

(b) Encourage international co-operation in the production, exchange and dissemination of such information and material from a diversity of cultural, national and international sources;

(c) Encourage the production and dissemination of children's books;

(d) Encourage the mass media to have particular regard to the linguistic needs of the child who belongs to a minority group or who is indigenous; and

(e) Encourage the development of appropriate guidelines for the protection of the child from information and material injurious to his or her well-being, bearing in mind the provisions of articles 13 and 18.

Article 18
1. States Parties shall use their best efforts to ensure recognition of the principle that both parents have common responsibilities for the upbringing and development of the child. Parents or, as the case may be, legal guardians, have the primary responsibility for the upbringing and development of the child. The best interests of the child will be their basic concern.
2. For the purpose of guaranteeing and promoting the rights set forth in the present Convention, States Parties shall render appropriate assistance to parents and legal guardians in the performance of their child-rearing responsibilities and shall ensure the development of institutions, facilities and services for the care of children.

3. States Parties shall take all appropriate measures to ensure that children of working parents have the right to benefit from child-care services and facilities for which they are eligible.

Article 19
1. States Parties shall take all appropriate legislative, administrative, social and educational measures to protect the child from all forms of physical or mental violence, injury or abuse, neglect or negligent treatment, maltreatment or exploitation, including sexual abuse, while in the care of parent(s), legal guardian(s) or any other person who has the care of the child.

2. Such protective measures should, as appropriate, include effective procedures for the establishment of social programmes to provide necessary support for the child and for those who have the care of the child, as well as for other forms of prevention and for identification, reporting, referral, investigation, treatment and follow-up of instances of child maltreatment described heretofore, and, as appropriate, for judicial involvement.

Article 20
1. A child temporarily or permanently deprived of his or her family environment, or in whose own best interests cannot be allowed to remain in that environment, shall be entitled to special protection and assistance provided by the State.

2. States Parties shall in accordance with their national laws ensure alternative care for such a child.

3. Such care could include, inter alia, foster placement, kafalah of Islamic law, adoption or if necessary placement in suitable institutions for the care of children. When considering solutions, due regard shall be paid to the desirability of continuity

in a child's upbringing and to the child's ethnic, religious, cultural and linguistic background.

Article 21
States Parties that recognize and/or permit the system of adoption shall ensure that the best interests of the child shall be the paramount consideration and they shall:

(a) Ensure that the adoption of a child is authorized only by competent authorities who determine, in accordance with applicable law and procedures and on the basis of all pertinent and reliable information, that the adoption is permissible in view of the child's status concerning parents, relatives and legal guardians and that, if required, the persons concerned have given their informed consent to the adoption on the basis of such counseling as may be necessary;

(b) Recognize that inter-country adoption may be considered as an alternative means of child's care, if the child cannot be placed in a foster or an adoptive family or cannot in any suitable manner be cared for in the child's country of origin;

(c) Ensure that the child concerned by inter-country adoption enjoys safeguards and standards equivalent to those existing in the case of national adoption;

(d) Take all appropriate measures to ensure that, in inter-country adoption, the placement does not result in improper financial gain for those involved in it;

(e) Promote, where appropriate, the objectives of the present article by concluding bilateral or multilateral arrangements or agreements, and endeavour, within this framework, to ensure that the placement of the child in another country is carried out by competent authorities or organs.

Article 22
1. States Parties shall take appropriate measures to ensure that a child who is seeking refugee status or who is considered a refugee in accordance with applicable international or domestic law and procedures shall, whether unaccompanied or accompanied by his or her parents or by any other person, receive appropriate protection and humanitarian assistance in the enjoyment of applicable rights set forth in the present Convention and in other international human rights or humanitarian instruments to which the said States are Parties.

2. For this purpose, States Parties shall provide, as they consider appropriate, co-operation in any efforts by the United Nations and other competent

intergovernmental organizations or non-governmental organizations co-operating with the United Nations to protect and assist such a child and to trace the parents or other members of the family of any refugee child in order to obtain information necessary for reunification with his or her family. In cases where no parents or other members of the family can be found, the child shall be accorded the same protection as any other child permanently or temporarily deprived of his or her family environment for any reason, as set forth in the present Convention.

Article 23
1. States Parties recognize that a mentally or physically disabled child should enjoy a full and decent life, in conditions which ensure dignity, promote self-reliance and facilitate the child's active participation in the community.

2. States Parties recognize the right of the disabled child to special care and shall encourage and ensure the extension, subject to available resources, to the eligible child and those responsible for his or her care, of assistance for which application is made and which is appropriate to the child's condition and to the circumstances of the parents or others caring for the child.

3. Recognizing the special needs of a disabled child, assistance extended in accordance with paragraph 2 of the present article shall be provided free of charge, whenever possible, taking into account the financial resources of the parents or others caring for the child, and shall be designed to ensure that the disabled child has effective access to and receives education, training, health care services, rehabilitation services, preparation for employment and recreation opportunities in a manner conducive to the child's achieving the fullest possible social integration and individual development, including his or her cultural and spiritual development.

4. States Parties shall promote, in the spirit of international co-operation, the exchange of appropriate information in the field of preventive health care and of medical, psychological and functional treatment of disabled children, including dissemination of and access to information concerning methods of rehabilitation, education and vocational services, with the aim of enabling States Parties to improve their capabilities and skills and to widen their experience in these areas. In this regard, particular account shall be taken of the needs of developing countries.

Article 24
1. States Parties recognize the right of the child to the enjoyment of the highest attainable standard of health and to facilities for the treatment of illness and

rehabilitation of health. States Parties shall strive to ensure that no child is deprived of his or her right of access to such health care services.

2. States Parties shall pursue full implementation of this right and, in particular, shall take appropriate measures:

(a) To diminish infant and child mortality;

(b) To ensure the provision of necessary medical assistance and health care to all children with emphasis on the development of primary health care;

(c) To combat disease and malnutrition, including within the framework of primary health care, through, inter alia, the application of readily available technology and through the provision of adequate nutritious foods and clean drinking-water, taking into consideration the dangers and risks of environmental pollution;

(d) To ensure appropriate pre-natal and post-natal health care for mothers;

(e) To ensure that all segments of society, in particular parents and children, are informed, have access to education and are supported in the use of basic knowledge of child health and nutrition, the advantages of breast-feeding, hygiene and environmental sanitation and the prevention of accidents;

(f) To develop preventive health care, guidance for parents and family planning education and services.

3. States Parties shall take all effective and appropriate measures with a view to abolishing traditional practices prejudicial to the health of children.

4. States Parties undertake to promote and encourage international co-operation with a view to achieving progressively the full realization of the right recognized in the present article. In this regard, particular account shall be taken of the needs of developing countries.

Article 25
States Parties recognize the right of a child who has been placed by the competent authorities for the purposes of care, protection or treatment of his or her physical or mental health, to a periodic review of the treatment provided to the child and all other circumstances relevant to his or her placement.

Article 26
1. States Parties shall recognize for every child the right to benefit from social security, including social insurance, and shall take the necessary measures to achieve the full realization of this right in accordance with their national law.

2. The benefits should, where appropriate, be granted, taking into account the resources and the circumstances of the child and persons having responsibility for the maintenance of the child, as well as any other consideration relevant to an application for benefits made by or on behalf of the child.

Article 27
1. States Parties recognize the right of every child to a standard of living adequate for the child's physical, mental, spiritual, moral and social development.

2. The parent(s) or others responsible for the child have the primary responsibility to secure, within their abilities and financial capacities, the conditions of living necessary for the child's development.

3. States Parties, in accordance with national conditions and within their means, shall take appropriate measures to assist parents and others responsible for the child to implement this right and shall in case of need provide material assistance and support programmes, particularly with regard to nutrition, clothing and housing.

4. States Parties shall take all appropriate measures to secure the recovery of maintenance for the child from the parents or other persons having financial responsibility for the child, both within the State Party and from abroad. In particular, where the person having financial responsibility for the child lives in a State different from that of the child, States Parties shall promote the accession to international agreements or the conclusion of such agreements, as well as the making of other appropriate arrangements.

Article 28
1. States Parties recognize the right of the child to education, and with a view to achieving this right progressively and on the basis of equal opportunity, they shall, in particular:

(a) Make primary education compulsory and available free to all;

(b) Encourage the development of different forms of secondary education, including general and vocational education, make them available and accessible to every child, and take appropriate measures such as the introduction of free education and offering financial assistance in case of need;

(c) Make higher education accessible to all on the basis of capacity by every appropriate means;

(d) Make educational and vocational information and guidance available and accessible to all children;

(e) Take measures to encourage regular attendance at schools and the reduction of drop-out rates.

2. States Parties shall take all appropriate measures to ensure that school discipline is administered in a manner consistent with the child's human dignity and in conformity with the present Convention.

3. States Parties shall promote and encourage international co-operation in matters relating to education, in particular with a view to contributing to the elimination of ignorance and illiteracy throughout the world and facilitating access to scientific and technical knowledge and modern teaching methods. In this regard, particular account shall be taken of the needs of developing countries.

Article 29
1. States Parties agree that the education of the child shall be directed to:

(a) The development of the child's personality, talents and mental and physical abilities to their fullest potential;

(b) The development of respect for human rights and fundamental freedoms, and for the principles enshrined in the Charter of the United Nations;

(c) The development of respect for the child's parents, his or her own cultural identity, language and values, for the national values of the country in which the child is living, the country from which he or she may originate, and for civilizations different from his or her own;

(d) The preparation of the child for responsible life in a free society, in the spirit of understanding, peace, tolerance, equality of sexes, and friendship among all peoples, ethnic, national and religious groups and persons of indigenous origin;

(e) The development of respect for the natural environment.

2. No part of the present article or article 28 shall be construed so as to interfere with the liberty of individuals and bodies to establish and direct educational institutions, subject always to the observance of the principles set forth in paragraph 1 of the present article and to the requirements that the education given in such institutions shall conform to such minimum standards as may be laid down by the State.

Article 30
In those States in which ethnic, religious or linguistic minorities or persons of indigenous origin exist, a child belonging to such a minority or who is indigenous shall not be denied the right, in community with other members of his or her group, to enjoy his or her own culture, to profess and practise his or her own religion, or to use his or her own language.

Article 31
1. States Parties recognize the right of the child to rest and leisure, to engage in play and recreational activities appropriate to the age of the child and to participate freely in cultural life and the arts.

2. States Parties shall respect and promote the right of the child to participate fully in cultural and artistic life and shall encourage the provision of appropriate and equal opportunities for cultural, artistic, recreational and leisure activity.

Article 32
1. States Parties recognize the right of the child to be protected from economic exploitation and from performing any work that is likely to be hazardous or to interfere with the child's education, or to be harmful to the child's health or physical, mental, spiritual, moral or social development.

2. States Parties shall take legislative, administrative, social and educational measures to ensure the implementation of the present article. To this end, and having regard to the relevant provisions of other international instruments, States Parties shall in particular:

(a) Provide for a minimum age or minimum ages for admission to employment;

(b) Provide for appropriate regulation of the hours and conditions of employment;

(c) Provide for appropriate penalties or other sanctions to ensure the effective enforcement of the present article.

Article 33
States Parties shall take all appropriate measures, including legislative, administrative, social and educational measures, to protect children from the illicit use of narcotic drugs and psychotropic substances as defined in the relevant international treaties, and to prevent the use of children in the illicit production and trafficking of such substances.

Article 34
States Parties undertake to protect the child from all forms of sexual exploitation and sexual abuse. For these purposes, States Parties shall in particular take all appropriate national, bilateral and multilateral measures to prevent:

(a) The inducement or coercion of a child to engage in any unlawful sexual activity;

(b) The exploitative use of children in prostitution or other unlawful sexual practices;

(c) The exploitative use of children in pornographic performances and materials.

Article 35
States Parties shall take all appropriate national, bilateral and multilateral measures to prevent the abduction of, the sale of or traffic in children for any purpose or in any form.

Article 36
States Parties shall protect the child against all other forms of exploitation prejudicial to any aspects of the child's welfare.

Article 37
States Parties shall ensure that:

(a) No child shall be subjected to torture or other cruel, inhuman or degrading treatment or punishment. Neither capital punishment nor life imprisonment without possibility of release shall be imposed for offences committed by persons below eighteen years of age;

(b) No child shall be deprived of his or her liberty unlawfully or arbitrarily. The arrest, detention or imprisonment of a child shall be in conformity with the law and shall be used only as a measure of last resort and for the shortest appropriate period of time;

(c) Every child deprived of liberty shall be treated with humanity and respect for the inherent dignity of the human person, and in a manner which takes into account the needs of persons of his or her age. In particular, every child deprived of liberty shall be separated from adults unless it is considered in the child's best interest not to do so and shall have the right to maintain contact with his or her family through correspondence and visits, save in exceptional circumstances;

(d) Every child deprived of his or her liberty shall have the right to prompt access to legal and other appropriate assistance, as well as the right to challenge the legality of the deprivation of his or her liberty before a court or other competent, independent and impartial authority, and to a prompt decision on any such action.

Article 38

1. States Parties undertake to respect and to ensure respect for rules of international humanitarian law applicable to them in armed conflicts which are relevant to the child.

2. States Parties shall take all feasible measures to ensure that persons who have not attained the age of fifteen years do not take a direct part in hostilities.

3. States Parties shall refrain from recruiting any person who has not attained the age of fifteen years into their armed forces. In recruiting among those persons who have attained the age of fifteen years but who have not attained the age of eighteen years, States Parties shall endeavour to give priority to those who are oldest.

4. In accordance with their obligations under international humanitarian law to protect the civilian population in armed conflicts, States Parties shall take all feasible measures to ensure protection and care of children who are affected by an armed conflict.

Article 39

States Parties shall take all appropriate measures to promote physical and psychological recovery and social reintegration of a child victim of: any form of neglect, exploitation, or abuse; torture or any other form of cruel, inhuman or degrading treatment or punishment; or armed conflicts. Such recovery and reintegration shall take place in an environment which fosters the health, self-respect and dignity of the child.

Article 40

1. States Parties recognize the right of every child alleged as, accused of, or recognized as having infringed the penal law to be treated in a manner consistent with the promotion of the child's sense of dignity and worth, which reinforces the child's respect for the human rights and fundamental freedoms of others and which takes into account the child's age and the desirability of promoting the child's reintegration and the child's assuming a constructive role in society.

2. To this end, and having regard to the relevant provisions of international instruments, States Parties shall, in particular, ensure that:

(a) No child shall be alleged as, be accused of, or recognized as having infringed the penal law by reason of acts or omissions that were not prohibited by national or international law at the time they were committed;

(b) Every child alleged as or accused of having infringed the penal law has at least the following guarantees:

(i) To be presumed innocent until proven guilty according to law;

(ii) To be informed promptly and directly of the charges against him or her, and, if appropriate, through his or her parents or legal guardians, and to have legal or other appropriate assistance in the preparation and presentation of his or her defence;

(iii) To have the matter determined without delay by a competent, independent and impartial authority or judicial body in a fair hearing according to law, in the presence of legal or other appropriate assistance and, unless it is considered not to be in the best interest of the child, in particular, taking into account his or her age or situation, his or her parents or legal guardians;

(iv) Not to be compelled to give testimony or to confess guilt; to examine or have examined adverse witnesses and to obtain the participation and examination of witnesses on his or her behalf under conditions of equality;

(v) If considered to have infringed the penal law, to have this decision and any measures imposed in consequence thereof reviewed by a higher competent, independent and impartial authority or judicial body according to law;

(vi) To have the free assistance of an interpreter if the child cannot understand or speak the language used;

(vii) To have his or her privacy fully respected at all stages of the proceedings.

3. States Parties shall seek to promote the establishment of laws, procedures, authorities and institutions specifically applicable to children alleged as, accused of, or recognized as having infringed the penal law, and, in particular:

(a) The establishment of a minimum age below which children shall be presumed not to have the capacity to infringe the penal law;

(b) Whenever appropriate and desirable, measures for dealing with such children without resorting to judicial proceedings, providing that human rights and legal safeguards are fully respected.

4. A variety of dispositions, such as care, guidance and supervision orders; counseling; probation; foster care; education and vocational training programmes and other alternatives to institutional care shall be available to ensure that children are dealt with in a manner appropriate to their well-being and proportionate both to their circumstances and the offence.

Article 41
Nothing in the present Convention shall affect any provisions which are more conducive to the realization of the rights of the child and which may be contained in:

(a) The law of a State Party; or
(b) International law in force for that State.

PART II

Article 42
States Parties undertake to make the principles and provisions of the Convention widely known, by appropriate and active means, to adults and children alike.

Article 43
1. For the purpose of examining the progress made by States Parties in achieving the realization of the obligations undertaken in the present Convention, there shall be

established a Committee on the Rights of the Child, which shall carry out the functions hereinafter provided.

2. The Committee shall consist of ten experts of high moral standing and recognized competence in the field covered by this Convention. The members of the Committee shall be elected by States Parties from among their nationals and shall serve in their personal capacity, consideration being given to equitable geographical distribution, as well as to the principal legal systems.

3. The members of the Committee shall be elected by secret ballot from a list of persons nominated by States Parties. Each State Party may nominate one person from among its own nationals.

4. The initial election to the Committee shall be held no later than six months after the date of the entry into force of the present Convention and thereafter every second year. At least four months before the date of each election, the Secretary-General of the United Nations shall address a letter to States Parties inviting them to submit their nominations within two months. The Secretary-General shall subsequently prepare a list in alphabetical order of all persons thus nominated, indicating States Parties which have nominated them, and shall submit it to the States Parties to the present Convention.

5. The elections shall be held at meetings of States Parties convened by the Secretary-General at United Nations Headquarters. At those meetings, for which two thirds of States Parties shall constitute a quorum, the persons elected to the Committee shall be those who obtain the largest number of votes and an absolute majority of the votes of the representatives of States Parties present and voting.

6. The members of the Committee shall be elected for a term of four years. They shall be eligible for re-election if renominated. The term of five of the members elected at the first election shall expire at the end of two years; immediately after the first election, the names of these five members shall be chosen by lot by the Chairman of the meeting.

7. If a member of the Committee dies or resigns or declares that for any other cause he or she can no longer perform the duties of the Committee, the State Party which nominated the member shall appoint another expert from among its nationals to serve for the remainder of the term, subject to the approval of the Committee.

8. The Committee shall establish its own rules of procedure.

9. The Committee shall elect its officers for a period of two years.

10. The meetings of the Committee shall normally be held at United Nations Headquarters or at any other convenient place as determined by the Committee. The Committee shall normally meet annually. The duration of the meetings of the Committee shall be determined, and reviewed, if necessary, by a meeting of the States Parties to the present Convention, subject to the approval of the General Assembly.

11. The Secretary-General of the United Nations shall provide the necessary staff and facilities for the effective performance of the functions of the Committee under the present Convention.

12. With the approval of the General Assembly, the members of the Committee established under the present Convention shall receive emoluments from United Nations resources on such terms and conditions as the Assembly may decide.

Article 44
1. States Parties undertake to submit to the Committee, through the Secretary-General of the United Nations, reports on the measures they have adopted which give effect to the rights recognized herein and on the progress made on the enjoyment of those rights:

(a) Within two years of the entry into force of the Convention for the State Party concerned;

(b) Thereafter every five years.

2. Reports made under the present article shall indicate factors and difficulties, if any, affecting the degree of fulfilment of the obligations under the present Convention. Reports shall also contain sufficient information to provide the Committee with a comprehensive understanding of the implementation of the Convention in the country concerned.

3. A State Party which has submitted a comprehensive initial report to the Committee need not, in its subsequent reports submitted in accordance with paragraph 1 (b) of the present article, repeat basic information previously provided.

4. The Committee may request from States Parties further information relevant to the implementation of the Convention.

5. The Committee shall submit to the General Assembly, through the Economic and Social Council, every two years, reports on its activities.

6. States Parties shall make their reports widely available to the public in their own countries.

Article 45
In order to foster the effective implementation of the Convention and to encourage international co-operation in the field covered by the Convention:

(a) The specialized agencies, the United Nations Children's Fund, and other United Nations organs shall be entitled to be represented at the consideration of the implementation of such provisions of the present Convention as fall within the scope of their mandate. The Committee may invite the specialized agencies, the United Nations Children's Fund and other competent bodies as it may consider appropriate to provide expert advice on the implementation of the Convention in areas falling within the scope of their respective mandates. The Committee may invite the specialized agencies, the United Nations Children's Fund, and other United Nations organs to submit reports on the implementation of the Convention in areas falling within the scope of their activities;

(b) The Committee shall transmit, as it may consider appropriate, to the specialized agencies, the United Nations Children's Fund and other competent bodies, any reports from States Parties that contain a request, or indicate a need, for technical advice or assistance, along with the Committee's observations and suggestions, if any, on these requests or indications;

(c) The Committee may recommend to the General Assembly to request the Secretary-General to undertake on its behalf studies on specific issues relating to the rights of the child;

(d) The Committee may make suggestions and general recommendations based on information received pursuant to articles 44 and 45 of the present Convention. Such suggestions and general recommendations shall be transmitted to any State Party concerned and reported to the General Assembly, together with comments, if any, from States Parties.

PART III

Article 46
The present Convention shall be open for signature by all States.

Article 47
The present Convention is subject to ratification. Instruments of ratification shall be deposited with the Secretary-General of the United Nations.

Article 48
The present Convention shall remain open for accession by any State. The instruments of accession shall be deposited with the Secretary-General of the United Nations.

Article 49
1. The present Convention shall enter into force on the thirtieth day following the date of deposit with the Secretary-General of the United Nations of the twentieth instrument of ratification or accession.

2. For each State ratifying or acceding to the Convention after the deposit of the twentieth instrument of ratification or accession, the Convention shall enter into force on the thirtieth day after the deposit by such State of its instrument of ratification or accession.

Article 50
1. Any State Party may propose an amendment and file it with the Secretary-General of the United Nations. The Secretary-General shall thereupon communicate the proposed amendment to States Parties, with a request that they indicate whether they favour a conference of States Parties for the purpose of considering and voting upon the proposals. In the event that, within four months from the date of such communication, at least one third of the States Parties favour such a conference, the Secretary-General shall convene the conference under the auspices of the United Nations. Any amendment adopted by a majority of States Parties present and voting at the conference shall be submitted to the General Assembly for approval.

2. An amendment adopted in accordance with paragraph 1 of the present article shall enter into force when it has been approved by the General Assembly of the United Nations and accepted by a two-thirds majority of States Parties.

3. When an amendment enters into force, it shall be binding on those States Parties which have accepted it, other States Parties still being bound by the provisions of the present Convention and any earlier amendments which they have accepted.

Article 51
1. The Secretary-General of the United Nations shall receive and circulate to all States the text of reservations made by States at the time of ratification or accession.

2. A reservation incompatible with the object and purpose of the present Convention shall not be permitted.

3. Reservations may be withdrawn at any time by notification to that effect addressed to the Secretary-General of the United Nations, who shall then inform all States. Such notification shall take effect on the date on which it is received by the Secretary-General.

Article 52
A State Party may denounce the present Convention by written notification to the Secretary-General of the United Nations. Denunciation becomes effective one year after the date of receipt of the notification by the Secretary-General.

Article 53
The Secretary-General of the United Nations is designated as the depositary of the present Convention.

Article 54
The original of the present Convention, of which the Arabic, Chinese, English, French, Russian and Spanish texts are equally authentic, shall be deposited with the Secretary-General of the United Nations.